Sarvepalli Radhakrishnan (1888-1975) is universally recognized as modern India's greatest philosopher. He was also a statesman of distinction, and even compared to Plato's ideal of the philosopher-king.

After a brilliant academic career, he taught at a number of Indian and foreign universities, including at Oxford University, where he was the Spalding Professor of Eastern Religions and Ethics, before being appointed as the Vice-Chancellor of Benaras Hindu University. From 1962 to 1967 he was the President of India.

'Among the philosophers of our time, no one has achieved so much in so many fields... Never in the history of philosophy has there been quite such a world-figure.'

George P Conger in *The Hindu*

By the same author

in

Orient Paperbacks

Adaptive Indian: Identity & Ethos

Religion, Science and Culture

Indian Religious Thought

Living with a Purpose

THE FOUNDATION OF CIVILISATION

IDEAS AND IDEALS

S. Radhakrishnan

Orient Paperbacks

DELHI | MUMBAI

Visit **www.orientpaperbacks.in** to read more about all our books and to buy them. You will also find features, author interviews, offers, and you can sign up for e-newsletter so that you're always first to hear about our new releases.

ISBN : 978-81-222-0052-2

The Foundation of Civilisation: Ideas and Ideals
(Originally published in 1936 as *Freedom and Culture*)

Subject: Philosophy

1st Published 1990
This Printing 2024

Published by
Orient Paperbacks
(A division of Vision Books Pvt. Ltd.)
5A/8 Ansari Road, New Delhi-110 002
www.orientpaperbacks.in

Printed and bound at Saurabh Printers, Noida, U.P.

CONTENTS

PUBLISHER'S PREFACE

Dr. Radhakrishnan is immensely readable for reasons more than one. He spells out India's ancient wisdom in modern idiom. The other-worldly philosophy and mundane science find a unique synthesiser in him. He does not sermonise, but urges the readers to pursue, discover and see truth face to face. His words enlighten the path towards a rational, balanced and meaningful life for one and all. His message focusses on the youth, in universities and colleges, help dispel the clouds of doubt and cynicism enveloping the academic world. He is able to revive the eternal values in the present context and re-establish the foundation of enduring human civilisation.

The essays published in the book are largely based on Dr Radhakrishnan's speeches to the university audiences, specially the students, in pre-independent India. Yet these do not read dated, and remain meaningful even today.

Our minds build cathedrals before the workmen have moved a stone; and our minds destroy them before the elements have worn down their arches.

Prof. Alfred N. Whitehead

No nation can stand still within its closed gates, while humanity is marching on.

CHAPTER 1

DEVELOPING THE HIGHER MIND: ITS CONSCIENCE AND ITS IDEAS

While the term 'university' is a modern one in India, it's meaning has been familiar to us for ages past. If the earliest records of India are to be trusted, we find the students gathered round famous teachers with strange enthusiasm and in surprising numbers. Takshasila, (now, Taxila, situated in Pakistan), the capital of Gandhara in northwest India the native land of Panini the grammarian, attracted fine young men from all quarters of India even as early as the fourth century B.C. The famous seats of learning belonging to Nalanda, Vikramasila, our own Dharanikota, Benares and Navadvipa were cultural centres to which flocked not only crowds of Indians but many eager students from distant parts of Eastern Asia.

The universities, the whole body of teachers and pupils had something like a corporate existence. These seats of learning were responsible for developing the higher mind of the country, its conscience and its ideals. They helped to produce what we might call a university world, a community of cultural ideas, a profound like-mindedness in basic aims and ideas.

In the altered circumstances of today, it is the universities that have to assume the leadership in the world of ideas and ideals. India and rest of the world, distracted by the deadly feuds of creeds and communities require more than ever the spread of the university spirit of self-criticism and broad-minded reasonableness towards the peoples' beliefs and practices. The *Shastris* and the Pandits, the Moulvis and the Moulanas, the Missionaries and the Clergymen of the conventional type are not likely to be of much help to us in our present condition. They seem to think that religion has come into the world in order to afford careers for pendants and priests, and not that the mass of men may have life and may have it more abundantly.

We are all familiar with the type of mind which is concerned with the protection of privilege. It upholds privilege by plausible arguments and employs in its defence the powerful motive of self-interest. It deludes itself into the belief that what the critics call privilege is but the law of nature, and the barest justice requires the satisfaction of its prejudices. But in some parts of the country the troubles are due to the opposite type of mind, the type which strives strenuously to obtain universal conformity to its own standards. The mind which works for conformity, shrinks at nothing to gain its ends. When inflamed by passion, it resorts to violence and persecution. To cast the whole of a great people in one mould and subdue them into the blind acceptance of a central power or creed is what we are taught to characterise as the Prussian method, though it is not peculiar to Prussia.

Conformity has been the dream of despots, political as well as religious. The ideal of the university is the promotion of liberty of mind or freedom of thought. It has little to do with the protection of privilege or a call to conformity. It contests privilege which is something other than that excellence which follows on intellectual eminence or spiritual greatness. It contests conformity, for each individual has the right to develop his own convictions. As a society of thinkers, the university is the home of liberty. The power and presence of the types of mind which deny liberty and uphold privilege or conformity are responsible for communal bigotry and religious fanaticism. It is the task of the university to break down these types of mind and reshape the thought and temper of the age.

The history of humanity is a ceaseless conflict between two fundamental instincts, the instinct of defence of conservatism which jealously clings to what it holds, turns back into itself and locks itself in; and that of expansion, the bubbling of life, of the vital urge that ceaselessly strives to break down the barriers. Every age of expansion is succeeded by one of contraction and vice versa. The age of the Vedic seers was a period of vigour and vitality when India gave voice to immortal thoughts. The great epic of the *Mahabharata* gives us a wonderful picture of seething life, full of the freedom of enquiry and experiment. New and strange tribes poured into the country and the *Mahabharata* relates how the culture was vigorous enough to vivify the new forces that threatened to stifle it and assimilate to the old social forms the new that came to expel them. In the age of the Buddha, the country was stirred to its uttermost depths.

The freedom of mind which it produced expressed itself in a wealth of creation in all phases of life, overflowing in its richness the continent of Asia. Chandragupta, the great military leader, almost unified a continent. Asoka, of immortal fame, sent

Buddhist missions to Syria and Egypt, Cyrene[1] and Epirus[2]. India soon became the spiritual home of China and Japan, Burma (now Myanmar) and Ceylon (now Sri Lanka). Under the Guptas and the Vardhanas, there was an immense cultural flowering. Those who carved deep out of the solid rock 'cells for themselves and cathedrals for their gods' which are even today the admiration of the world must have had sufficient strength of spirit. But soon the spirit of creation died away. The vivid life, the passionate enthusiasm and the strong conviction gave place to teachers less original, to ambitions less exalted and to tame compliance with the old forms. There was a dread of venturing outside the safe limits of guaranteed ideas. The country seemed to suffer from exhaustion. The ebb of the tide had reached its utmost. At the present moment, we are in one of those periods when humanity, pushed back by the powers of reaction, is about to make a great leap into the future. Everywhere the same suffocation is felt, the same vital need to pull down the walls, to breathe freely, to look around on a vaster horizon.

If the institution of university is to participate in what may fittingly be called the Indian Renaissance, it must pay adequate attention to the study of India's past. This land of ours is no sand bank thrown up by some recent caprice of earth. It is a stately growth with roots striking deep through the centuries. Nations have a history as well as a geography. They live and grow, not by the forces of wind and rain, sun and stars, but by the passions and ideals which animate them. The universities must stimulate an interest in the sources of our civilisation, its art and thought, its language and literature, its philosophy and religion. Any one who has studied and meditated on the ancient classics

---

1 Cyrene: The ancient Greek city (founded about 630 BC), situated in present day Libya.

2 Coastal region of northwestern Greece and Southern Albania.

of this country will testify to their peculiar greatness, their power to yield new meanings and their inexhaustible value as a criterion of present-day modes of life. In these days of startling scientific developments, it may not be useless to point out that reconstructing the mosaic of the long forgotten past is not a less ennobling performance on the part of the human mind than calculating the movements of the stars or making ships fly in the air.

To plead for an awakened interest in Indian culture is not to advocate a return to the conditions of antiquity. The past never returns. In the European Renaissance of the 15th and 16th centuries, there was a renewal of interest in the thought of Greece and Rome and the early Christian church, and it marked the beginning of modern European civilisation. So I believe a study of our past will lead to a quickening of our cultural life and a triumph over scholasticism.

In the handling of the past of one's country, there is one serious danger which we have to guard against. We are tempted to look for great things in the past which is generally regarded as a golden age of peace and plenty, when men lived for centuries, married angels and entertained gods. The farther we go into the past of a country, the greater is the temptation to the uncontrolled imagination. The danger is a very subtle one to every real interpreter of history. If he is to present his work in an intelligible way, he must note the general principles unifying the multitude of facts with which he deals. It is but a short step from perceiving this unity to imposing the design of one's own making. We must beware that we do not give more than their due weight or value to the facts observed. To pervert the past in order to gain new sanctions for our dreams of the future is to sin against our intellectual conscience. If a scientific study of the past of India is possible, it is only in the atmosphere of a university.

A discriminating and critical study of the beliefs and institutions of our country is fitted to be much more than a means of satisfying an enlightened curiosity and of furnishing material for the researches of the learned. It is a powerful instrument for progress. History is a mirror in which we may see ourselves, not merely our outer forms as in a common glass but, if only we choose, our inner selves, stripped of trappings and spread out on the table. We can find our strength as well as our weakness, the gems of life, growth and recovery as well as the maladies which afflict us. We can discover why we, the products of a civilisation which has lasted for nearly forty centuries, are only half alive today. We live and yet do not. Why is it so? If we are to be restored to health and vigour, we must learn to conquer our national failings.

We must find out what those institutions are which have outlived their utility and still survive, thanks to our mental laziness and the extreme unwillingness to overhaul habits and beliefs that have become automatic in their workings. To the conservative mind and the artist soul it may appear a melancholy task to strike at the foundations of beliefs in which, as in a strong temple, the hopes and aspirations of a large section of humanity through long ages have sought a refuge from the strain and stress of life. It is difficult to break even physical habit, it is much more difficult to break long established habits of thought and mind. But I hope that love of ease, regard for antiquity or considerations of safety will not induce us to spare the ancient moulds, however beautiful, when they are outworn. It is not true conservatism, but a false sentimental one, which tries to preserve mischievous abuses simply because they are picturesque. Whatever comes of it, wherever it leads us, we must follow truth. It is our only guiding star. To say that the dead forms which have no vital truth to support them are too ancient and venerable to be tampered with, only prolongs the suffering of the patient who is ailing from the poison generated by the putrid waste of the past. We need not shy at change. Our philosophy tells us that permanence belongs to eternity alone and unceasing change is the rule of life.

It is impossible for any nation to stand still and stiff within its closed gates, while humanity is marching on. The world is no more a miscellaneous collection of odd and dislocated spots where we could live alone. It has become a small neighbourhood where we can neither live alone nor be let alone. We cannot return to the walled cities of the middle ages. The flood of modern ideas is pouring on us from every side and will take no denial. On the question of response to the new forces, there is much confusion of thought. We come across a curious blending of self-assertion and timidity. There is a passionate loyalty to everything Indian haunted by deep but secret misgivings. The conservatives adopt an attitude of forlorn resistance and cling tenaciously to old ideas. They little realise that the forces will steal unknown, bring down the defences where they are weak and cause inward explosion. The radicals are anxious to forget the past; for, to them, it is to be remembered, if at all, not with pride but with shame. But they forget that where other cultures may give us the light, our own furnishes the conditions for action. The constructive conservatism of the past is the middle way between the reactionary and the radical extremes.

If we study the history of Indian culture from the beginning of its career, somewhere in the valley of the Indus four or five millenniums ago, down till today, the one characteristic that pervades it throughout its long growth is its elasticity and ability to respond to new needs. With a daring catholicity that approaches foolhardiness on occasions, it has recognised elements of truth in other systems of thought and belief. It has never been too proud to learn from others and adopt such of their methods as seemed adaptable to its needs. If we retain this spirit, we can face the future with growing confidence and strength.

The recovery of the old knowledge in its depth and fullness, its restatement in new forms adapted to present needs, and an original handling of the novel situations which have arisen in the light of the Indian spirit, are urgent necessities and if our universities do not accomplish them, nothing else will. I hope that the universities will give an important place to Indian culture in its schools of humanities. It is needless to say that its special task would be to present to the world an authentic account of the history based on literary, artistic and historic records. Sanskrit literature, the Epics and the Puranas will be of considerable value in such an undertaking. I hope the University will make the study of a classical language compulsory for all students at some stage or other of the arts' course.

I am aware that we are anxious to give greater attention to our mother tongue and make it, if possible, the medium of instruction and examination in the degree courses as well. This very desirable reform has to be worked out with great caution. English is not only the language of international commerce and thought, but is also one of the chief factors in the making of the Indian nation. If the course in English is not of a sufficiently high standard, our students are likely to be at a disadvantage in their search for posts which, after all, is not a minor consideration. India is not the only country in the world where we have to pay regard to the commercial value of a university career.

While we look to the humanities for the development of the inner spirit, which is necessary for any sound national reconstruction; sciences, pure and applied, will help us to build the outer organisation. A passionless and understanding contemplation of objective. Nature is in itself an intellectual satisfaction of a high order. The scientific temper is characterised by a passion for facts, careful observation and cautious statement of conclusion. It discourages reliance on vague impressions, second-hand evidence and hasty generalisation. It is quite possible in these days of specialisation that our graduates might obtain their degrees without the knowledge of a single objective science. I hope the Academic Council will make such a thing impossible by providing for the compulsory study of an objective science by the arts' students at the stage of the Matriculation, if not the Intermediate.

We live in an age of intense striving and creative activity. If we are to be credited with intellectual power, we cannot afford to say, 'let others make the experiments, we will benefit by their experience.'

The assumption that we are metaphysically minded and are not interested in the pursuit of science is not quite true. In our vigorous days, we developed sciences like astronomy and architecture, mathematics and medicine, chemistry and metallurgy. Latterly, however, there has been a decline in scientific activity owing to the cramping effects of scholasticism. All signs indicate that we are waking up from our scientific slumber. The work done in the post-graduate schools of the Calcutta University shows that our men are competent to do original work of a high quality, if only they have the opportunity. If we are to swing out again into the main stream of the life of the world, universities must build laboratories and equip them adequately thus offering opportunities for original investigation to the abler students of science.

I hope there are not many who sneer at the conquests of science as materialistic avenues to the betterment of human conditions. A spiritual civilisation is not necessarily one of poverty and disease, man-drawn rickshaw and the hand-cart. It is one thing to say that wisdom is more precious than rubies and the wise man is happy whatever befall him, and quite another to hold that poverty and ill-health are necessary for spiritual advance. While poverty is spiritual when it is voluntary, the crass poverty of our people is a sign of sloth and failure. Our philosophy of life — reorganise the production and increase the wealth — are among the legitimate aims of human endeavours. Pursuit of wealth does not in itself spell spiritual ruin. It is a means, in itself, ethically colourless, neither good nor evil, but a necessary means for the attainment of the higher life for the individual and the mass of mankind. What counts is the purpose for which wealth is striven after, and so long as we realise that it is a means to a higher end, we can boldly venture out on the path of the conquest of Nature's secrets and their utilisation for man's service. There are so many ills that flesh is heir to, which need not be met by fatalism and folded hands. Instead of facing suffering and disease by apologetic justifications of the ways of god to man, a nobler piety demands their reduction and ultimate removal.

Economic crises are slow and undramatic. As we cannot visualise the coarse poverty of the large majority of our people, our emotions react to it rather sluggishly. The average standard of material well-being is exceedingly low; poverty is widespread and is causing immense unhappiness, though it is not for the most part the fault of the poor. Middle class unemployment is growing apace. Industrial and commercial activities, to which educated young men of other countries devote themselves, exists at low levels. Young men from five years of age upto twenty are trained in our educational institutions and at the end of all the toil and the cost, find themselves faced by blind alley occupations and unemployment. It is a tragic waste of human effort in a country where so much needs to be done. Earth and its resources are bountiful and there are plenty of hands capable of producing wealth and yet they are all lying idle.

It is not fair to contend that Indians are unwilling to apply themselves to industrial pursuits as they are more speculative than practical. There does not seem to be anything radically wrong about the Indian mind. Till the industrial revolution, the conditions were practically the same in India and in Europe. Our agricultural methods, economic institutions, industrial developments and the relations between the landlords and the tenants were governed on almost the same lines in India as in Europe. Only we happen to remain still in large parts, in the medieval agrarian and pre-industrial stages. This is a matter for deep concern.

* * *

An educational policy over-weighted on the literary side on account of its inexpensive character is largely responsible for the wrong notions of the dignity of certain callings and indifference to others. It is not more dignified to hold a pen and keep accounts than to work in a factory or a field.

It is very much to be hoped that the State will give up the narrow view of its functions as a super-policeman maintaining law and order and in a larger spirit foster the industrial growth of the country and help India to find her feet in the world. It is not fair to condemn lack of private initiative and enterprise, for State socialism prevails to a large extent in the country. Industrial development is obviously not the direct concern of the universities. Technical education will have to depend on the creation of industries, which does not lie in the hands of the universities. But with the goodwill and co-operation of the State, the universities can help the industrial growth of the country by the institution of new technical courses which will have a direct relationship to Indian industries.

Academic opinion, the world over, is against purely examining and affiliating bodies. The main function of a university is not to grant degrees and diplomas, but to develop the university spirit and advance learning. The former is impossible without corporate life, the latter without honours and post-graduate schools.

While many students join the university for its utility rather than for its culture, still when once they are in, they should find themselves in a community of workers devoted to the pursuit of knowledge for its own sake. This is the old Indian ideal of *gurukulavasa* carried out on a larger scale. The university is not so much the official lecture room where the teacher gives a set lesson to his pupils, as the atmosphere where the new generation first becomes conscious of itself, where reputations, sometimes life-long, are made in private discussions in somebody's room.

I am not much in sympathy with the idea of developing the sciences in one centre and the arts in another. The liberal arts and the pure sciences complete, correct and balance each other. Recent events in England and America have shown the enormous importance of scientific evolution for philosophy and religion.

Lord Haldane in his Bristol address on the 'Civic University' observes: 'You cannot without danger of partial starvation separate science from literature and philosophy. Each grows best in the presence of the other.'

Subjects like Experimental Psychology and Anthropology are closely related to both art and science. Only the other day we requested a distinguished professor of Physics to explain to our philosophy men in Calcutta (now Kolkata) the principles of Einstein's relativity. The students will be the gainers by living in a University where all subjects are taught, though each may pursue only a few of the subjects. In these days of specialisation, it is difficult for one to keep oneself up-to-date in any branch of learning without neglecting to a certain extent other branches of learning. University life, where men pursuing learning in different spheres daily meet together in intellectual and social intercourse, is the only safeguard against the dangers of over-specialisation.

The value of university training consists not so much in the information acquired as in the scientific habits developed. The student should learn to distinguish knowledge from opinion, fact from theory, should be able to weigh evidence, argue closely and state and examine fairly the opponent's point of view. The spirit of research is nothing else than the carrying out of this attitude of free enquiry and rational reflection. Whether a university succeeds in this, its chief aim or not depends on its staff of professors. It is the men who fill the chairs that create the atmosphere. We cannot be over careful in the selection of professors. No other consideration should weigh with us in the appointment of professors than academic achievement and original work, for where there is no zeal for research there is no zest in teaching.

The Andhra University has for its motto a great saying of the Upanishads *Tejasvinav adhitam astu*. May our study impart that inward light or *tejas*! May it grant us the power (*virya*) to stir the soul to effort! If you are truly educated, you will have the light to see the truth and the strength to make it prevail. Young men and women of today have a greater opportunity to show their real worth than at any other time in our recent history.

The great light (*tejas*) which shall also be an actuating power is what we need, the light that tells us, in the famous words of Lamartine: 'No man ever riveted a chain of slavery round his brother's neck but God silently welded the other end round the neck of the tyrant.' Unfortunately it is the case that the ardent advocates of modernism in public life are at the same time staunch devotees of medievalism in social life and habits. There cannot be substantial political advance or industrial growth unless we develop corporate life and comradeship. No power on earth can stand against the corporate effort of a people to recover its manhood. The difficulties of the enterprise, far from being a reason for giving it up in despair, are to my mind a reason for accepting it as the challenge of the age. Education and discipline and constant forbearance alone can help us.

We Indians are fortunately situated in some respects. The hold of conservatism is not strong. Our generosity of spirit and openness of mind are well known. Our social instinct and suggestibility are still active. Our moral sense and sympathetic imagination are not much warped by dogma. Our women are relatively more free. Love of the mother tongue binds us all Hindus, Muslims and Christians. If the universities supply a constant stream of young men and women imbued with love of truth and of service to man, it will help to bring about a renaissance, not only an intellectual renaissance but a moral and spiritual one.

May it be your endeavour to realise the poet's dream that in this land all may be in a position to overcome the difficulties of life, to attain an insight into the good, to gain wisdom and find enjoyment anywhere.

Sarvas taratu durgāṇi, sarvo bhadrāni paṣyatu,
Sarvas tad buddhim apnotu, sarvas sarvatra nandatu.

We cannot offer to you any glittering prizes of wealth or position or power. You have only difficulties of an unheard of character to face. May God give you the courage and the insight, the self-sacrifice and the devotion which alone can make you worthy to fulfil the task before you.

Culture of the soul is the first and the fairest thing that the best of man can ever have.
— Plato

CHAPTER 2

CULTURE OF THE SOUL: FREEDOM OF THE MIND

It is said, with truth, that the function of a university is to prepare the young to take their place in human society. It must provide its members with the knowledge and skill necessary to make them efficient citizens. But is the whole duty of man exhausted by the acquisition of knowledge and professional training? Is a university only an institution for higher learning, a factory which turns out clerks and technicians able to run the machinery of the State? Mere knowledge which gratifies curiosity is different from culture, which refines personality.

Culture is not remembering a mass of curious details about the dates of birth of the great heroes of the world or the interesting names of the fastest ships which cross the Atlantic or entertaining odds and ends gathered from the latest *Who's Who.* A well-known institution of this country has for its motto *sā vidyā yā vimuktaye;* that is knowledge which is designed for salvation, for the development of the soul's best. Such an idea is not merely an Indian idiosyncrasy. Plato said long ago that the culture of the soul is 'the first and fairest thing that the best of men can ever have.' According to Goethe, the object of education is to form tastes and not simply to communicate knowledge. A man's culture is not to be judged by the amount of tabulated information which he has at his command, but by the quality of mind which he brings to bear on the facts of life.

Education is not cramming the mind with a host of technical details, putting sight as it were into blind eyes. The eye of the soul is never blind; only its gaze may be turned to the false and the fleeting. Too often the vision may be dragged downwards by the 'leaden weights' of pride and prejudice, of passion and desire. The function of the teacher is not to add to the 'leaden weights' but remove them and liberate the soul from the encumbrances so that it may follow its native impulse to soar upwards. The student at a university does not merely learn something, but becomes something by being exposed, in the most elastic period of his life, to transforming influences, such as the constant clash of mind with mind, the interchange of ideas, the testing of opinions and the growth of knowledge of human nature.

A university is a fellowship of spirits, a society of seekers of truth who believe that there are things in life of vastly greater importance than wealth and comfort, necessary as these are. It affirms that the pursuit of ideas and inspirations is greater than the race for power and glory. To belong to a university is to share this way of looking at things and feeling about them, to acquire this largeness of view which can assuage the asperities of life. Culture is born of meditation on the best that has been said and thought on the intimate problems of life, in the university which is a retreat from the crowded world, for solitude and study. A man into whose soul there has passed in some small measure the soul of great literature and art, philosophy and religion, will find a significance in life that would otherwise be hidden from him. He will develop an inner grace of nature, a tendency of the soul which makes him live in constant and confident communion with the unseen, even when tormented by earthly passions.

Culture is the transformation of one's being, the alteration of the psychology of man. It is thinking with one's whole mind and body. It is making one's entire organism, sense and sensibility, mind and understanding, thrill with the idea. Donne's beautiful lines about the blushing girl describe the oneness of the human being:

Her pure and eloquent blood
Spoke in her cheeks, and so distinctly wrought
That one might almost say her body thought.

'Her body thought.' The whole organism can think and thrill. Man is not to be mistaken for a merely intellectual being. The ideas framed by our intellect must sink into the sub-soil of our life and leaven our whole nature, conscious and unconscious. Only then does the word, the thought, become flesh. That we can grow wise without effort, is a soothing dream. Wisdom comes through austere meditation, through the inward travail of the spirit. The dreams and the suggestions that flit before us must possess us, dominate us, transform us, recreate us. Light must become life. There is a legend that ghosts do not speak until they drink blood: even so, our noble dreams do not become facts of life except through the blood of our hearts. Culture is what produces the sweetness of temper, sanity of mind and strength of spirit.

To avoid misunderstanding, I may say that cultural value is not a special quality of 'arts' subjects. The spirit and the method in which a subject is taught determine its cultural value and not the nature of the subject itself.

One of the early writers on education, a certain Richard Recorde writes in *The Castle of Learning* (1556) that astronomy should be an essential part of education for it will moderate human pride and self-importance and fill the mind with a sense of the majesty of God. A century later, Descartes said to one who approached him for advice about the daily conduct of life: 'Begin every day by meditating for a few minutes on the majesty of God as displayed by the mighty works of his creation.'

We cannot scan the heights and sound the depths of the universe without being impressed by the profound mystery of it all. The writings of Jeans and Eddington breathe a spirit of intellectual modesty. Some of the essential elements of culture, desire for accurate knowledge and intellectual sincerity, are fostered by scientific studies. The duty of truth-seeking 'demands of us — surrender of prejudices and sacrifice of sympathies as dear to one as life itself.' The obligation for intellectual sincerity is something which no university student can escape from. Truth or repose, it has been said, you may take which you please, you never can have both. Safety first cannot be the maxim of a university. In a country like ours, the need for scientific studies is much greater than the most modern of us may think. If we are to battle with ignorance and suffering, we must be up-to-date in our methods of fight.

Science has done more for the emancipation of the masses than the wisdom of the sages. It is erroneous to assume that happiness is enjoyed only by those who are desperately poor. It is idle to pretend that poverty is better than wealth, malnutrition than nutrition, foul air than fresh air. Simplicity is not the same as squalor. Again, we have a tendency to use words without weighing their meanings. Science will help to free us from the tyranny of words, by taking us to things themselves. The triumphs of science which have enabled mankind to establish civilisation over chaos declare the majesty of the human spirit quite as much as artistic achievement.

While I am second to none in my appreciation of the value of science, pure and applied, for our country, it is essential to combine with its study a synoptic view of the whole. The effort and the concentration necessary to master even a small part of the sphere of knowledge are so great that no one can master the whole of it. Every student of a university should, however, know in a general way the things that give value, meaning and dignity to human life, the arts and pursuits that give man his vocation in this planet. A university fails of its purpose, if it does not in some small measure help us to gain an ample outlook on the realm that surrounds us, the realm of nature with its wondrous order, the realm of human experience with its vast tracts of human history and the aspirations of men who have made them memorable, the realm of the unseen to which, in the course of ages, new and ampler meanings have been steadily opening out. A mind at peace with itself is one of the essential ingredients of a happy life, and a university course is not complete if it does not afford its members the scope to put their mental house in order and arrive at some knowledge of themselves and their place in the universe. In a well-known school of technology in the United States, there is a compulsory course on metaphysics for all its students. Dr McTaggart of Cambridge used to give weekly lectures on the general problems of philosophy open to the members of the university.

The passion for political freedom is running high. But, like everything else, freedom is won from within and not given from without. The country we love is not a geographical area but a spiritual possession. Until we identify ourselves with it through mind, heart and will, wisdom, love and service, sanity, sweetness and strength, our country is bound to be in its present intolerable condition. The forces we have to contend against are more within our borders. Our lack of ordinary human interest in communities other than our own, our unthinking adoption of practices and prohibitions, our social tyranny which makes cowards or automata of most of us, our religious fanaticism, are wrongs which require immediate attention. The advancement of social understanding and the promotion of the spirit of service and sacrifice are ideals which a university must think worthy of its high calling. Ability to co-operate with others is the true test of education, among individuals as well as communities, and it is possible only with sweetness and humanity. If we are to assist human beings in sorrow to bear the anguish they are called upon to endure, we have to approach them with feeling and sympathy, with love and understanding.

The great majority of altruistic minded people feel satisfied about themselves, when they become members of social reform associations or subscribe to the funds of fellowship clubs. But man reveals himself to man in love and sympathy and not in answer to questionnaires or in mental clinics. The human soul yearns for warm love and is repelled by cold curiosity. If we go through a day with calm and serenity, understanding the hearts of men and women we come across, instead of working up statistics at office desks or distributing pamphlets in public meetings, we will effectively help the betterment of the social order. Reconstruction of the world will follow if we undertake the less exciting but more exacting task of reconstructing one-self by purifying the passions and humanising the self.

The universities have been a very inefficient guide if they have not disturbed our more or less blind faith, if they have not developed the mood of reflective inquiry. In our country, however fast we may try to efface them, the truces of antiquity are all about us. The earth's surface is not raw but subtly moulded by old time. No nation can grow if it has not its roots in the past.

We cannot start an entirely new civilisation; we might as well try to build a new tree. We have to work within the general limits imposed by the past, which no power on earth can undo.

The spirit of the past can be gathered from the history of the people. If we go to Indian history in order to learn and not inflict on her our own petty prejudices, we find there not a fixed programme, but a continuing spirit. The creative tradition, the living past, is like a seed that grows and not like a log of wood. We are not obliged to bless every stage and example of it. It is a waste of time to revive the forms of ancient life in the modern world. If Manu were read for practical guidance today, it were better for us that Manu had not been born. The scriptures of an earlier age cannot answer the problems of our time. We must not hesitate to extract the vital principles of universal value from what is strictly local and temporary. Absorbing the lessons of centuries, we must accept the intimations that are reaching us still.

The great representatives of Indian culture were men of mobility and ceaseless adventure and we are not loyal to their spirit if we mark time in a world of perpetual movement by sitting still and chanting ancient hymns. We cannot command the Sun to stand still in the plains of Hindustan, searching the scriptures while the storm was blowing, half ruining the country. 'What my father did is good enough for me,' is the maxim of the decadent; that no man can be his own ancestor is the principle of the progressive. Our primary duty today is to face facts as we find them, even though they may hurt our national pride and remember in dealing with them the principal truths of all religions, which are, roughly speaking, the universality of spirit, the inviolability of personality, the fact of fellowship, the duty of service and the power of sacrifice.

Culture is not culture if it does not produce the type of mind which will never assist intellectual or social tyranny. The cultured ones are the free spirits of the world. Humanism has been the fundamental assumption of Indian culture. The world is one family. The ideal sage of ancient India is one who exclaims: 'While there is a soul in prison, I am not free; while there is an enslaved community, I belong to it.'

While humanism has been the essential key-note of Indian culture, nationalism seems to be the most potent force in our time. It is not India that originally propounded the maxim: 'My country, right or wrong,' or produced the psychology that one's country is always right. The tremendous urge of the nationalist movement is the direct result of Western influence. Our men trained in the history of Western nations and taught for years that nothing is more precious than freedom, that freedom is not only necessary but more essential than anything else, seem to have learnt the lesson. We cannot expect them to read the stories of Thermopylae and Salamis without emotion. We cannot construe the march of Garibaldi from Palermo to Naples as a walking exercise round the fort. At a time of life when impressions are freely received and assimilated, when the world has brought no disappointment to love or frustration to endeavour, when the appeal of idealism is intense and the gates of the future seem wide open, our young men and women read the history of the freedom movement in the West.

It is not a matter for surprise that their imagination is thrilled and their aspiration kindled. They discover that the civilisation of the ancient Hindus and the Greeks developed in an atmosphere of freedom. It is no accident that progress in knowledge and scientific activity in modern Europe coincides exactly with the centuries which have marked a loosening of the grip of authority on the mind of man. When the human mind is enslaved by tyranny of any kind, we have a dark age. Contact with the West has roused in us the sense of pride and self-respect and contributed largely to the Indian Renaissance. The two currents, the Eastern and the Western, the Asiatic and the European, emphasising as they do, though not exclusively, inward security and outward efficiency have met face to face in India. Nowhere else do we find such close contact and interchange between the two systems. As a result of this process which is still in progress we may be able to reach principles more comprehensive in their scope and able to meet the complex needs of modern life.

The Indo-British association merely is the outer expression of the ultimate synthesis between the East and the West. A firm political connection secured by common interests, a sound economic interchange and mutual industrial helpfulness on healthy lines, a new cultural relationship between two most important sections of humanity, Europe and Asia, in which they could exchange all that is vital and valuable as equal members of the human household, a close partnership in the building of a new and rich culture for the life of a nobler humanity is an ideal worth striving for. But smaller minds interpret the British connection in a more sordid way. If empire means markets for the central power, men, money and munitions for planting the flag in the extremes of the world, if it means the massing of troops in a variety of colours against similar groupings on battle fronts, if it means the exploitation of the weak and the backward, such an empire is a vulgarity, a reaction, a danger to the peace of the world. If the larger objective prevails, if goodwill and sympathy govern Indo-British relations, the Commonwealth will become more enduring. The bonds of friendship are a defence more solid than soldiers and machine guns.

For the Indian mind, ideas are more potent than facts even though the ideas may be illusions. The Indian thinks and feels in terms of national pride and self-respect. He stresses the shame of subjection and the lines of sorrow which even the best Indians bear in their faces. While the British seem to exaggerate the demands of security, the Indians emphasise the right to liberty. Security and liberty do not always coincide. Are we to have the maximum freedom consistent with the maximum safety? That is the problem. While conflicts of interests can be composed by reason and argument, conflicts of passions produce fear and suspicion, which make all peaceful solutions difficult. The problem can be solved only by that sympathetic understanding of another's point of view and by that true statesmanship, which steadily looking to the future avoids stressing the obstacles which loom so large in the path of the mere politician whose eye and whose ear are on the ground only one step in advance of his feet.

It is a privilege to be alive today. History is being made before your eyes. Everything is on the move. Nothing is settled. You will live to see changes, political and social, greater than any which have taken place in our country within living memory. It is the duty of intellectuals to give an informed and decisive lead to the people. It is no use adopting an attitude of laziness on the comfortable view that institutions are not made but grow, and difficulties which seem too thorny for timid fingers to touch will settle themselves by being left alone. If we leave society to reform itself the whirlwind will come on us. It is your duty to plan and build wisely. Remember in all your activities the central principle of all good life:

Sruyatām dharmasarvasvam srutvā caivāvadhāryatām
ātmanaḥ pratikūlāni pareṣāṃ na samācaret.

It is my earnest wish that the sons and daughters of India may increase in virtue, learning and numbers, and go forth into the world equipped with knowledge, filled with culture, servants of the Ideal.

To foster a type of mind that does not take the usual for granted, that does not believe that its ways of thought and life are a part of eternal order of nature. A mind that is young in spirit.

CHAPTER 3

ESSENCE OF EDUCATION: DEVELOPING AN ADVENTUROUS MIND

The universities were founded in pursuance of the policy of the Government to encourage unitary and residential universities in which unofficial social contacts count far more than official lectures and examinations. An understanding of life fostered by the social and athletic activities, by the clash of personality, by the interchange of opinion, by the testing of views, is more important than even intellectual gifts. Understanding does not mean learning or skill, but what the French proverb suggests: 'to understand all is to forgive all'. It helps to feel the complexity as well as the mystery of life. There is so much in it of which we know little.

The man of understanding does not profess to have an opinion on everything and does not sum up an author in a phrase or a civilization in an epigram. He has the openness of outlook, the freedom and flexibility of thought, the capacity to imagine other states of mind. His mind possesses space and air and is thus free from dogmatism and is ever ready to sympathise with views which it does not share. Understanding in this sense is what enables our thoughts and desires to be subordinated to a chosen end, what makes life yield its full significance.

Understanding is not something which can be measured by the tape or weighed in the balance and delivered to the students by the members of the faculty at the Convocation ceremony. It is a contagion that one catches. The ancient symbolised culture which is acquired in a college to a torch that is passed on from hand to hand down the generations. This lighted torch is a dangerous gift. It has stirred many an upheaval, started many a conflagration. It symbolises the spirit of revolution, the cleansing fire which burns the wood, hay, and stubble that have come down to us. If we are afraid of the upturnings of the soil, of the social, economic and political upheavals consequent on the spread of this fire, we should not go near a university. We may as well shut it down.

If university education is to enable us to anticipate needs and meet new situations, it should not be hampered by obsolete thought and tradition. An educated man is not one who lives in petrified illusions but is released from the burden of inert ideas. He preserves the sense of wonder and curiosity and his mind is fresh and adventurous. The spirit of a university is the spirit of youth.

In Plato's *Timaeus* we read that one of the Egyptian priests who was of a very great age said: 'O Solon, Solon, you Hellenes are but children, and there was never an old man who was a Hellene.' Solon in return asked him what he meant. 'I meant to say,' he replied, 'that in mind you are all young: there is no old opinion handed down among you by ancient tradition, nor any science hoary with age.'

The Greeks had no venerated classics or hoary books to check their free speculation. They never suffered from the weight of the past. Somewhat the same idea underlies the Sanskrit saying: *Vimarśa rūpiṇī vidyā*. The sense of discrimination, the spirit of criticism is the essence of education. The university has to foster the type of mind that does not take the usual for granted, that makes conventions fluid, that does not believe that its ways of thought and life are a part of the eternal order of nature. A mind that is young in spirit has the saving grace of scepticism. It has confidence in its capacity to face the new. If a university produces men who are low spirited, who play for safety, care for comfort, are afraid to take any risks, then that university has failed in its essential task. If it takes hold of the young with all the fullness and ardour of their youth and turns them into timid, selfish, conservative men, if it petrifies their ideas and freezes their initiative, the university has failed as a university.

It is the duty of man to move on. He is a born adventurer. 'Here have we no continuing city but we seek one to come.' It is a common delusion to assume that our young men are free thinking and that they are delivered from the bondage of authority and tradition, that each young graduate is working out a new code and devising a new creed for himself. I wish it were so, but nothing of the kind is happening. The modern mind is singularly servile to its teachers and leaders. It will believe almost anything it is told. It is intellectually timid and prefers to take its opinions from others. Every demagogue is bailed as a newly discovered prophet, and the latest fashion is welcomed as new revelation. Our young men are not able to resist appeals to their passions and prejudices and in many cases we find that their voice of reason is hushed and their vision is clouded by the appeal to selfish claims and interests. Timidity and conservatism are the general habits of mind and they are the greatest dangers to society. The classical age of Greece terminated, as we all know, with a 'failure of nerve.'

There are brief periods in the life of individuals, decades in the history of peoples, which through the intensity of the emotions they produce and the results they achieve are worth centuries of ordinary life. India is passing through such a historic period. The passion for political freedom is the greatest ferment at work. Even the left wing politicians would not care to deny the immense services rendered to this country by the early British administrators who established peace and security in territories which were frequently subjected to the ravages of contending hosts. But it would be equally futile to overlook the loss of self-respect and manhood of the nation incident to foreign rule. The present condition of mental and moral decay consequent on political subjection and economic depression is engaging our attention.

The study of Western history and institutions has roused in us a love of freedom and a sense of self-respect. Love of liberty is a native instinct of the human soul. Freedom is not coveted as a means for any further end of efficiency of administration or economic prosperity. It is not a means to any other end, it is itself the highest end.

Lord Acton in his *History of Freedom in Antiquity* (1877) says:

> *'A generous spirit prefers that his country should be poor and weak and of no account but free, rather than powerful, prosperous, and enslaved.'*

A nation has the right to gain experience of self-government even at the price of less efficient government. The strong desire to embody the ideas of freedom and self-determination in definite political institutions has become a burning passion owing to a number of factors of which the chief are the poverty of the country, middle class unemployment, low literacy, high death rates, costly civil administration, a heavy military budget and the Great War fought avowedly for the principles of freedom and self-determination. Every country in the world exhorts its citizens to buy its own goods and it cannot be a crime if we encourage our own industries. If our leaders demand that we should control our own political and economic affairs, it is the natural result of the policy of Great Britain in this country.

The first essential for achieving political freedom as well as for guarding it when attained is a juster social order. We must build a social structure rooted in principles of truth, freedom and equality. The university men are both the builders and the material of the new structure, and if they go out of the university and enter life imbued with honesty and the spirit of adventure, with vision and courage, they will help us to build the new India which is yet to be.

There are periods in the life of every country when the interests of the whole demand the sacrifice of private claims. The European nations in the Great War lived in one of such periods when their citizens set aside their individual comforts and interests for the sake of the national well-being. It is not true that such periods occur only when nations are threatened by external enemies. When a flood or a famine overtakes a land; a situation arises when the interests of the whole country dominate those of the individuals who compose it. To my mind, our country today is faced by a crisis of the first magnitude. It is not war or revolution or national bankruptcy but internal disruption that is threatening us. The new India which we are attempting to build is being strangled at its very birth by anti-national forces.

In the hour of our awakening we find ourselves surrounded by forces which make for our continued bondage. The failure to reach a communal settlement has had grave reactions. Faith, security and hope are displaced by a new distrust, a new anxiety, a new uncertainty. We have lost the spirit of courage and experiment associated with progressive nations. Mighty nations in the past had been doomed to decay because they could not change in response to changed conditions. History found them useless and swept them aside in its onward march. If we are to preserve ourselves, we must use the lighted torch, the cleansing fire, the spirit that rebels. We must wrestle with the past that oppresses us, the relics of barbarism that threaten our very life, the fantastic notions about elemental facts that militate against decent living. We do things in our daily life which are a disgrace to our humanity. We eat food, wear clothes, and enjoy comforts, while those who produce them are dying by degrees in unhealthy surroundings and bad economic conditions. We repress our natural sympathy with those who suffer, because it does not pay us. An acceptance of large-scale injustice is the price we pay for our comforts. We applaud an aberration which denies human rights to millions of our kith and kin, and, to our lasting shame, we confound it with religion.

Your education has been in vain if you are not protected from the dangers of dogmatism. No opinion is true simply because it is handed down from the past, and we cling to it with passion. It does not become more true simply because we have it in our power to impose penalties on those who refuse to accept it. The spirit of democracy is opposed to that of dictatorship. It does not matter whether it is of the religious or of the political type. If we are truly democratic, we will understand that it requires all sorts to make a world and we need not think that those who differ from us in their religious views go straight to hell.

We must have the humility to admit the value of the contributions which others make, however, remote they may be in their inner gifts and mental outlook from us. The tragic incidents of Kanpur, Dacca, Chittagong, and the anti-national movements show that we are still medieval in our mind and outlook, however much we may agitate for a constitution on the twentieth century model. In the middle ages, the church was the recognized custodian of the whole life of man, secular and religious. But if the church lords of modern Europe attempt to continue the same tradition and enact laws regarding the seemly length of a woman's skirt, they will be laughed at, and yet ordinances no less amusing are taken more seriously even by our educated men, and, in pursuance of them, we do not hesitate to fight with each other. The priestly classes still occupy a dominant position in our social order or, may I say, disorder. So long as we are unable to resist their influence and continue to think that the caste or the community matters more than the country, we are medieval in our minds and are unfit for true democracy. If we do not check this growing menace, we shall drift back into barbarism. The aspirations and disabilities are common to all classes and communities. If we suffer from insufficient nourishment, lack of due care for health, lack of work and rest under healthy conditions, they are not the monopoly of any class or community. Let it not be said, when the history of the freedom movement in India comes to be written, that any section, Hindu or Muslim, Sikh or Christian, betrayed the cause of the country for the sake of its own selfish gain.

We hear on all sides about the revolt of youth. I am afraid I have a good deal of sympathy with this attitude of revolt, and my complaint is that it is not sufficiently widespread. The general tendency to regard our ancient civilisation as idealistic and the modern one as materialistic is not the expression of revolt but of reaction. It is specious rationalisation in defence of our conservatism. There is nothing idealistic about disease or poverty, nothing spiritual in a system that uses human beings as beasts of burden. There is nothing materialistic about the application of science to the relief of human distress or the promotion of human happiness. The future seems to be with the youth who rebel against a corrupt social order and religious fanaticism. Those who are indifferent when the situation is so grave are guilty of cruelty. Injustice thrives on the indifference of the people. The bad employer, the unjust law, the corrupt leader, the false teacher thrive, because they have never been challenged. The unjust prevail because those who have a sense of justice suffer from inertia. If you have the imagination to visualise the amount of suffering, physical and mental, which a half-clothed and half-starved people undergo, you cannot be indifferent.

The spirit of revolt against the wrongs of society is not to be confused with indiscipline or intolerance. It is quite consistent with deep inward courtesy and a consideration for the feelings of others. We need not surrender fundamental good manners which are essential in every form of civilised society.

Many of our leaders aim not at truth but at success. They colour facts to suit their prejudices. We have studied with profit the methods of crowd suggestion and are employing them to deceive the ignorant. When you step out of the university and enter life, you are tempted to say what you are expected to say and not what you really think. It will be your task to discriminate between wise and dangerous leadership, between a competent, constructive, courageous one which looks to the future and a wasteful, destructive one which clings to the past.

The older generation will soon pass away and you will step into the breach. You will have unique opportunities of showing your worth. You will be called upon to fight the strongholds of ignorance and selfishness by hard thinking and bold effort. You cannot hope to drift on a tide of patriotic emotions into a readymade Utopia. You will have to prepare for a new order by hard work and hard thinking. You will not fail the country at a time when it stands in need of your service and guidance, if you remember the ideals which your university has put before you and stand up for courage and justice, truthfulness and fair play.

Time will show whether you are anxious for ease and comfort or truth and suffering, whether the university has developed in you qualities of courage, determination and self-denial or made you into snobs much too respectable, much too self-satisfied, much too ease-loving and afraid to do anything. Will you help India to break her bonds or will you bind them faster? Will you make out in your lives that it is a libel against you to say that a life of service and suffering has less attraction for you than a career of comfort? Time will answer.

Every great achievement is a vision in the soul before it becomes a fact of history.

CHAPTER 4

ESSENCE OF EDUCATION: THE POWER OF IDEAS

Graduation is only a milestone in life's journey. It does not mark the end of the educational road. In a very real sense, it is the commencement time, the beginning of a new journey which will test the toughness of your mental and moral fibre, the efficiency of your university training. The new experiences, the new problems and the new situations will demand from you the exercise of qualities for whose fostering the university functions. It does not require a prophet to say that India will rank as a free dominion in a short time.

The future will give large powers and responsibilities to you. The historic role of the educated classes in the building up of a new India cannot be over-estimated. If a leader is one who knows where he is going, who has a firm grasp of the insights and intuitions which have made our civilisation so enduring, and who can harness them to every aspect of life, it is only the universities that can train men for leadership. The universities are more than institutions for higher learning and professional training; they are called upon to educate the younger generation, form its character — create a new type of intellectual leader.

It is obvious that education has failed you if it does not develop in you a love of severe and sustained thinking, a power of resistance to popular sentiment and mob passion. An educated person will be willing to follow truth wherever it leads him and will refuse to be forced into action simply because everybody else is doing it. He knows that in knowledge there is power, that truth shall make for freedom. To build a new India we must think deeply and plan wisely. Creation is an act of faith, an act of renewal and hope, rendered possible by a new vision. 'Our minds build cathedrals before the workmen have moved a stone; and our minds destroy them before the elements have worn down their arches,' says Professor Whitehead. Every great achievement is a vision in the soul before it becomes a fact of history. If it is true that facts dominate life, it is equally true that facts themselves obey the force of mind. Ideas control the world. They will triumph over the blind forces. For dynamic conceptions which will remodel society, we must turn to the scholars and thinkers in the universities.

Never was a time when there was more need for hard thinking than in the present hour. We see on all sides a seething mass of turbulent life. We are faced with a situation produced if we can imagine it, by a combination of varied movements which the European nations passed through during the last few centuries. The intellectual renaissance, the industrial revolution, the political struggle for freedom and democracy and the religious reformation, which the Western nations faced individually and at different periods, India has to meet simultaneously, each magnified on account of the large area and population concerned.

While great changes are taking place in every side of life, political and industrial, cultural and social, there is a good deal of loose and muddled thinking. The country seems to be marching forth into the unknown.

A casual visitor may feel that nothing interests Indians so much as politics. The deep questions which have engaged us down the ages are practically forgotten. There is a general disposition to despise cultural interests, and make of life a rougher and ruder thing than in the spacious past. I do not deny that there is a good deal to be said for the preoccupation with politics. The stress of the struggle for the bare physical necessities is more formidable than it ever was. Bernard Shaw says that a subject nation is like a man suffering from cancer. He can think of nothing else. He will listen to all quacks who will profess to treat him. The teaching of the West is mainly responsible for the political unrest. It has been the explosive energy, the social dynamite. The political tradition derived from the ancient city-states of Greece has taught us a passionate love for free citizenship and a juster social order. We have learnt that the government without the consent of the governed is the very definition of slavery.

The aim of government is not so much efficiency as education. It is to afford training and opportunities for self-government. Muscles waste if they are not used; sinews become rigid if they are not stretched. Impetuous youth with its eager straining after the new vision chafes at every delay. We seem also to have learned from the West that success justifies all methods, and service to the nation excuses moral shortcomings. Such a view of political morals is not quite compatible with the tradition that cruelty is a crime for which there is no forgiveness. Nationalism means that we should do everything in our power to preserve our soul, our honour and integrity, and maintain our individual style of dealing with problems. We want freedom to preserve ourselves and make our distinctive contribution to the progress of the world. We cannot do so if we surrender our individuality. We must not try to make for ourselves an English or a Russian soul, but must extract from these whatever will serve to enrich our spirit. We can profit only by that which we are able to transform into our substance.

It is however the fact that there is a good deal of loose thinking on this question. In the minds of many of our leaders the antagonism to British rule is strangely mixed up with a love of British institutions. They are more anxious to westernise our country so as to make it a replica of Europe. Even the criticisms of Western institutions are inspired by Western thinkers like Karl Marx and Tolstoy, Romain Rolland and Bertrand Russell. We are violently Western in some moods and violently Indian in others. We are transitional creatures burdened with uncertainties, with chaos in our minds. The silent struggles in the souls of men are of greater importance than the spectacular ones on the political arena. Unfortunately the universities whose function is to control and organise fundamental thinking on basic issues seem to be suffering from inertia and indifference.

In the social and cultural realms the situation is not very different. We seem to swing between the two extremes of pride and self-contempt, constantly looking over our shoulders to see what others are about, wretched and anxious lest we make of ourselves a laughing stock. We are ashamed of the running sores in our body-politic and yet bewildered as to how we could remove them. The protective garment of tradition has become a thing of shreds and patches. The abstract rationalism of the revolutionary would make a clean sweep of the past; the equally abstract historicism of the reactionary would make a clean sweep of the present. Our inward unity is lost. The integration of social, cultural and political forces is broken up. And what shall a university education profit us, if it does not restore the unity and synthesise the old and the new?

It is easy to be romantic about the good old days. But it is a sure sign of decadence if we live contentedly in the traditional fabric of ideas congealed into forms. In the flux of life, the past is not the present. Progress is marked by originality and adventure; decay by imitativeness and routine. However perfect the wisdom of the past may be, the forms in which it is clothed are not final. They require to be broken and made afresh. We must recover the spirit of life and convert it to fresh purposes. The spirit of people is to be found not in what it was in past ages nor even in what it is now. As we survey the history of a nation, we get it at something deep and foundational, something which is for ever forming itself anew, though it never reaches perfect expression.

The spirit of people can only be defined in terms of this growing ideal, this operative principle which is very imperfectly expressed in any specific stage, though clearly discernible when we study the several stages in their temporal succession. The secret of life is in the law of development. In India the main emphasis has been on the reality of the life of spirit in man and the cosmos as a whole, and a search for truth wherever it may be found. India has always stretched out her hands towards the developments of life. It is only the recovery of the true spirit that will help to loosen the hold of the complicated and unnecessary trappings. The wood, hay and stubble that have come down to us must be consumed in order that the things which are not shaken may remain.

This work of discriminating between the permanent and the transitory in our tradition can be done only by the educated classes who have sufficient respect for the past and trust in the present. Our education is a failure if we do not obtain such a conception of the universe round us, such an understanding of the movement of life and the progress of mind as to secure for us a vision of spirit in every detail of nature and life, the spirit in which all human souls, the humblest and the greatest, live, move and have their being. The aim of education is not simply to enrich the minds of people with new knowledge, but also help them to rise to their full spiritual stature. It must rouse them to the value of spiritual realities, turn their eyes from the things which are merely temporal to the things which are eternal; and enable them to pursue the values that are ultimate and not be occupied with merely utilitarian ends. Such an education will make us ashamed of our narrow creeds and inflexible faiths which make even social relations difficult. Ability to co-operate with others is the true test of education among individuals as well as communities.

The state is the citizen writ large, according to Plato. If we live under an irresponsible government, it is more our fault than our misfortune. The kind of government under which we live is, on ultimate analysis, a reflection of ourselves. The Greek orator declared that 'It is not walls but men who make a city'. It is not so much physical geography as intellectual community that moulds a nation. The sense of like-mindedness and community of interests is required to be fostered if the feeling of nationality is to be furthered. Universities can stimulate common interests only if they are allowed to work in an atmosphere of freedom. It is a peculiarly difficult task for the universities to steer clear of dictation by the State and agitation by the people. The world over there is a tendency for political opinions to become rigid dogmas. Communism in Russia is a religion and individualism is infidelity. When the States assume the rigidity of churches, it becomes the primary duty of universities to protect us from the propaganda of the States themselves. In a country where the universities are endowed by the State, they require to be particularly careful and keep above all parties of religion and politics.

The universities must influence the whole generation and combat the sectional movements that are clogging our progress. They must cater to the educational needs of those who cannot like ordinary students enter their walls. An extra-mural department may well arrange single lectures or courses in suitable centres and institute diplomas in special studies. If the dangers of an industrialists' autocracy or a relapse into obscurantism are to be averted, an intensive programme of education will have to be adopted.

Culture is not mere learning. It is discrimination, understanding of life. Liberal education aims at producing moral gifts — as well as intellectual, sweetness of temper as much as sanity of outlook. Into the art of living, the cultured man carries a certain grace, a certain refinement, a certain distinction which redeems him from the sterile futility of aimless struggle. Culture is not a pose of intellect, or a code of convention but an attitude of life which finds nothing human alien, common or unclean. An education that brings up a young man in entire indifference to the misery and poverty surrounding him, to the general stringency of life, to the dumb pangs of tortured bodies and the lives submerged in the shadows is essentially a failure. If we do not realise the solidarity of the human community, nor have human relations with those whom the world passes by as the lowly and the lost, we are not cultured. The most deprived individual has his startling interest and the worst criminal is unique to his thumbprints as he knows to his cost. Great literature shames us out of our complacency and reveals to us something of the immense capacity of the human soul for suffering and isolation. We may suffer, we may fail, we may be forgotten but we have succeeded in the true sense of the term, we refused to be vulgar, mean or squalid. If anything justifies life, it is nobility, greatness. Man notices our failings, but God sees our strivings.

In our country today, we are suffering from want of understanding. Whether it is between the Indian and the British or the Hindu and the Muslim, we are up against the same difficulty. Even when we seem to understand each other, we suddenly reach a point where it becomes clear that we do not have a sufficient grasp of each other's meaning. The trouble is not so much with regard to high philosophy and art as with practical affairs and political motives. Understanding of human relations and motives is not a matter of scientific method which can be taught in a university. It is a contagion of the spirit, not analysable or demonstrable and yet it is not incommunicable. A good deal in this matter depends on the teachers and their outlook on life as distinct from their intellectual equipment. The unique experience of pursuing common ideals within the walls of the university in spite of differences of temperament and creed, has consequences of wider import. The many pleasant friendships, many personal contacts must not merely be vivid recollections but must remain with us to the end of our lives. It rests with you to pledge yourselves to one another, that, when misunderstandings and disputes arise, you will be among those who will counsel patience and restraint and proclaim that reason, fairplay and listening to both sides are the solvents of all differences.

Matthew Arnold spoke of sweetness and light as the marks of culture. We may add to them a third, strength. Sweetness of temper, sanity of outlook and strength of spirit, patience, wisdom and courage are the qualities of a cultured mind. There is a legend that ghosts do not speak until they drink blood; even so our noble dreams do not get accomplished except through the blood of our hearts. It is through *tapas*, through the inward travail of the spirit, that anything great can be achieved.

The Upanishad says, that supreme actualises mighty possibilities through the force of *tapas.*

> *Sa tapo tapyata, sa tapas taptvā idam sarvam asrjata.*
>
> 'He performed tapas: having performed tapas, he produced all this whatsover' (*Taitriya Upanishad* II. 6).

The best work in the world is achieved by those who resign the prizes of the world and bear in pain the burden of defeated hopes. The Rishis of ancient India knew no fear and feared no death. Buddha walked out of his palace to suffer and recreate. Christ is the man of sorrows. None who has not suffered to the utmost gets to the foundations of reality. In this matter of suffering we men are amateurs: but our women friends are the professionals. In the recreation of a new India, their share will be considerable.

I want to lay special stress on the need for suffering and strength, as I suspect that a kind of new materialism has overtaken us. We seem to be coddling with comforts and are willing to use all our intellectual resources ruthlessly in the service of one end, material success. We are prepared to lay down our lives for higher wages and not higher ideals. We seem to have almost a superstitious reverence for material conditions.

Times of transition require a new simplicity of life, a new asceticism; and you, to whom leadership in thought and practice is passing, need it most. We have no glittering prizes of wealth, power or glory to offer you but only hardship, struggle and suffering. May the ideals of the university help you to face them with spirit and courage and save you from cynicism and despair.

Let your resolve be one, let your heart be of one accord, let your minds be united that your assembly may be happy.
— Rig Veda, X 191, 2 and 4

CHAPTER 5

ART OF LIVING TOGETHER

If a State is to endure, said Aristotle, it must educate its youth in the spirit of its constitution. History abounds in illustrations of this dictum. Political changes are generally bound up with educational ones. The new ideas which recent years have brought to triumph in European as well as Asiatic countries are consolidating their position in educational institutions. Today a great change is being effected in the mind and temper of our people. New hopes are kindled, new prospects are opened before them. The right of the common man to be master of his fate is declared with a new emphasis. This new spirit which is at work in our country is still far from pervading our whole life. It is not yet triumphant in our educational institutions.

If the universities are to become instruments of social regeneration, they must help to sweep away the deep social cleavages which our traditional codes are concerned to uphold and prepare the youth for the new order. The new spirit, to my mind, consists in an increased emphasis on the application of science to human affairs and the development of social solidarity.

You are not departing from the right university ideals in embarking on a scheme of technological education. Preparation for livelihood is, in a sense, preparation for life. From the beginning, our university courses have been influenced by the demands of the public services and professions. A vocational bias, in a large sense, has always been with us. Many European countries, France and Germany, Belgium and Denmark, are also engaged in training their young men for life's work. One of the chief causes of unemployment in our country is the lack of the application of science to agriculture and industry. Only the other day, pointed attention was drawn to the appalling character of the unemployment problem, when over four thousand applications were received for thirteen vacancies in the Income-tax department. In the early days of university education, the graduate was a member of a leisured class with special opportunities for official employment, and unfortunately this bias still clings to the university student who expects on graduation a career in public service or the learned professions.

Men who have little natural capacity for theoretical studies such as law and literature, politics and philosophy, take to them and the intellectual powers which ought to be devoted to the improvement of life and material conditions for the mass of the population are spent in an unhealthy scramble for access to the professions which are overcrowded. The universities produce men who are incapable of being absorbed by the services and when their ambitions are not fulfilled, they are tempted into paths which are a danger to the State. The university graduates have thus become a difficult social problem. To some extent the excessive theoretical emphasis of Indian universities is responsible for it. The provision for the study of natural sciences, engineering and agriculture, whose scientific study is peculiarly vital to the welfare of India, is inconsiderable.

It does not, however, follow that technological education will cure unemployment. Even today there are men who in spite of the high technological training which they have acquired from foreign universities, are unable to secure suitable work. Our economic life, where there are few large scale industries, does not offer many openings for men with technical training. But the backward condition of our economic life is not so much an excuse for neglecting scientific and technological studies as a powerful reason for developing them. After all, business and industry, however undeveloped they may be, are less congested with trained talent in search of employment than are the civil service, politics, teaching, etc. Besides, with the increasing pressure of public opinion on the government of the country, I have no doubt that the government will be obliged to pursue a policy of increasing industrialisation. It is a matter for concern that almost 70 per cent of the population in India is dependent on agriculture and its allied occupations, whereas the corresponding figures for the other countries range from 10 per cent in UK to 35 per cent in Canada.

It is unfortunate that, while other countries of the world have been steadily pursuing a policy of progressive industrialisation, no such change is visible in India. The progressive States of the world are dealing with the problems of trade and industry. It is the duty of the leaders of the people to induce the government to adopt a bold system of planned economy as in Soviet Russia. We are not making such a success of our economic life that we can afford to ignore these exceedingly interesting experiments. Though we might reject the methods and institutions by which the communists have sought to realise their dreams, the Russian experiment raises an important issue which cannot be evaded. The ruin of the middle classes and the degradation of the proletariat into a pauper rabble has before now destroyed great nations. While it may not be wise to abolish private property altogether, it is necessary to transform the rights and responsibilities which attach to the ownership of it.

While it is not for the universities to improve agriculture or organise industries, it can undertake research in those subjects and provide the country with the technical experts required for its industrial development.

But scientific effort alone cannot take us far. The dangers which threaten civilisation today are traceable to the failure to make a rightful use of the enormously increased productive powers with which science has supplied us. There does not seem to be any check to the continuous prostitution of scientific effort to destructive purposes. The possibilities of the abuse of power are much greater today than in 1914 and if the spirit of man is not altered, a repetition of the calamity of 1914 may well threaten the extinction of civilisation. Our future depends less on the increasing powers with which science endows us than on the way these powers are employed by us.

The increasing unemployment and poverty side by side with greater productive power and fuller control over Nature have suggested to many that the objection of the manual worker to machinery is not ill-founded. But it is not machinery that is at fault, but man, the user of the machine. Science may develop in us readiness to face change, adaptability, accuracy of observation, honesty of thought and openmindedness, but they are not enough. Our quality of imagination must be roused and we must have an inspiring vision of the reign of justice and fair play on earth such as only poets and philosophers have dreamt of. It alone can lift us out of the common ruts of thought and action, in religion and social organisation. Those who help us to secure confidence in the values of spirit also make contributions to civilisation, quite as constructive and practical as leaders of science and captains of industry. Those who secure for us the vision of a new order of society and help us to emerge from the ignorance and brutality of a merely science-bred civilisation and realise the splendid powers of life are also our benefactors. Religion and philosophy, art and literature, help us in these things of the spirit.

Anyone who looks with intelligence and understanding at the times through which we are passing cannot help asking, what is one going to make of these rapidly moving, many-sided, complex changes, which affect every form and institution of life? There has been nothing like it in the recorded history of this country. We were not exposed at any previous period of our life, to such an amazingly varied and complicated series of influences and happenings that seem to twist our thoughts and feelings, our ideals and aspirations and challenge our very foundations.

It is not enough to have the institutions or instruments of democracy, but we should also find ready to hand the spirit of democracy. We have to promote the unity of aim and the solidarity of sentiment which will help individuals to sink personal or group advantages for the common good. Democracy is the recognition that it takes all sorts to make a world. It implies the humility which admits that others remote from ourselves in mental outlook and experience have also something of value in them. Whatever may be our race or language, religion or occupation, we are all necessary for the highest welfare of our country. Democracy is only social good manners.

A vastly extended franchise is bound to rouse unmeasured aspirations after social status and opportunities for mental development. Though we may formally emancipate women and depressed classes from their disabilities, they will in a true sense be unfree so long as the conditions of mental freedom are not put within their reach. I may give you an illustration of how futile mere constitutional changes are. 'The right of citizens of the United States to vote shall not be denied or abridged by the United States or by any State on account of race, colour or previous condition of servitude.' It is not possible, one would imagine, to guarantee more assuredly to the African American his exercise of the full electoral franchise than by this clause, written into the Federal Constitution in 1870 as its Fifteenth Amendment. And yet we know that such a clear provision of the Fundamental Law has been stultified in practice. Formal declaration of political equality or constitutional provisions are not enough. Political equality can be sustained only if opportunities for self development are granted to communities formally enfranchised.

Mahatma Gandhi raised his great voice in a powerful appeal to us to rise to new heights, to seek new means of progress and to tread new paths towards national reconstruction, greatness and accomplishment. He touched the foundations of society by pleading for a union of hearts, a fostering of communal unity without which power is a phantom and freedom a farce. We know how much opposition his call to remove untouchability is receiving. Many of us are still the slaves of custom and live in terror of the new and the unexpected. The majority of the ills from which we suffer are due to the sincere beliefs of good men and women. A sort of benevolent incredulity of the new characterises even some of our university men. Loyalty to usage is a self-protective virtue which we employ to guard our stupidity and preserve our ignorance. We cannot blame the fanatic, but we have to remove the causes, mental and moral, which make fanaticism popular.

The reactionary character of religion is responsible for the growing secularism. Religion seems to be the maker of its own misfortunes. Its hostility to all inquiry, its fanatic opposition to change make it a suspect on every side. It is not anything peculiar to Indian religions. As long ago as the days of the Old Testament, David felt that he had 'sinned greatly' in numbering Israel (2. Samuel, XXIV); but his followers today know how completely baseless his fears were. The use of anaesthetics in childbirth was condemned as contrary to the will of God by the persons of the last century. And the same arguments are used today against new methods of social hygiene and eugenics. There was a press message that the Archbishop of Naples had stated publicly that the recent Italian earthquake in which many unfortunate people lost their lives was God's way of showing that he disapproved of the obscenity of woman's dress. How exactly the Archbishop know that the divine protest was directed against feminine fashions and not fascist rule is not quite clear. The opposition to the removal of untouchability is not grounded in better foundations and the religious beliefs which trouble us so much today on such questions will not retain ere long more than pathological interest.

It is a period of instability and chaos that we are living in. Traditional beliefs are challenged, old lines are crumbling and new influences are pouring on us. A radical readjustment of fundamental ideas is the need of the hour. If we are to build up an appropriate and autonomous system of life and polity, we have to look far into our own background and find out the spirit of our country, those intangible forces and invisible values coming down the centuries. It is they which have given us this life in which we find ourselves, however difficult and desperately hard it may be. Some of our leaders in their disgust with the dictatorial insolence of obscurantism may feel that the past is a hindrance to progress, that it simply hinders our memory, distracts our attention and often blinds us to the significance of the present.

The very weight of the past seems to isolate us from the living present.

While it is often necessary for us to forget 'those things that are behind', we cannot completely break away from the past. If we know individuals who suffer from loss of memory, we will understand what a complete break with the past means in the way of bewilderment and incapacity for daily living. A man is not himself without his memory. What is true of individuals is true of peoples. Even as the nations of the West transformed themselves by making use of the cultural wealth of antiquity at the time of the Renaissance, we have to follow the same laborious path by extracting from our own history and philosophy the equivalents of the intellectual conditions in which European nations found themselves at the time of the Renaissance. No civilisation which has developed in another land and in different conditions can become ours. We have to link up our new effort with our past, use the spirit and method rather than the result of the Western science and criticism to fertilise our own culture. Only thus can we produce a specific Indian contribution to the collective wisdom of the world.

Such a critical appreciation of the past and fruitful integration of the old and the new can take place only if we adopt an attitude of respect for the past tempered by criticism. Many of us suffer from the infantile complex of self-glorification and forget that corporate humanity is as necessary as personal modesty. We cannot ignore the obvious fact that we are today low-spirited, lacking in spring, ill at ease in the world. A modification of the influences of the past is essential. We cannot revive the ancient forms in the modern world. It is no use repining idly over the beauty of the broken fragments or turning aside from the stream of modern life to admire in detached contemplation the perfection of a vanished past. We have to recapture the spirit of life in the past and convert it to fresh purposes. We have to take hold of that inner core, that secret spirit, which though not strictly definable continues constant amid the mutations of circumstances. If it has any vitality, it must grow with the ages, inspiring new ends and yielding new discoveries. If we cling to it, we will be enabled to loosen ourselves from the choking hold of the complicated trappings of life, combat the blunting of individual freedom and development by the superstitions of the past. The discerning students of India's past have to give a new hope and a new impulse to all those who are today stifled by the medieval atmosphere. If the chains that fetter the human spirit are to lose their power to impede and imprison, the university will have to study the ancient classics without pedantry or partisanship and secure free play for ideas. They cannot do this, if they are themselves filled with dust and convention and not endowed with life and creative power.

It is the function of the university to produce not only scholars with the prophetic vision, but also leaders of the new democracy. Democracy is not rule by a rabble or a caucus. It is not submission to mass opinion or obedience to dictators. There is no finer definition of democracy than that of Mazzini, who said that, 'It is the progress of all through all under the leadership of the wisest and best'; 'the wisest and best', not merely the best born. We want leaders who are not anxious to keep their seats of leadership but who are prepared to tell the truth and guide us to a right solution of our problems. There is a temptation for an uneducated or half-educated democracy to put in places of power men of forensic ability, political dexterity or money power; such a temptation is difficult to overcome unless the electorate has intelligence and ability, public spirit and independence, qualities which cannot be got to order.

The universities can provide us with men of disciplined courage, men who will be directors and not merely exponents of public opinion. It will not do in these troublous times to play for safety, demand secure careers and look out for soft options. If you expect them, you will be disappointed. You must be prepared to go out of conventional grooves and take chances in life and be ready to do anything worth doing. Youth, if it is not anaemic or fossilised, will always be adventurous in thought and action. The message I leave with you is, preserve the spirit of youth, of adventure and of courage. Equip yourselves for the new era of social harmony and progress of which you can in your own way be the creators. That ancient scripture of India, the *Rig Veda* which was composed when the earth was young, impresses on us the need for social unity, the need for renouncing our personal advantage for the sake of the common good.

> *Saṃgacchadhwaṃ saṃ vadadhwaṃ saṃ vo manāṃsi jānatām.*
>
> Together walk ye, together speak ye, together know ye your minds.
>
> *Samanī va ākūtiḥ samānā hrdayāni vaḥ*
> *Samānam astu vo mano yathā vaḥ susahāsti.*
>
> Let your resolve be one, let your heart be of one accord, Let your minds be united that your assembly may be happy.
>
> — *Rig Veda, X, 191, 2 and 4*

There can be no social stability without social justice.

CHAPTER 6

JUSTICE AND EQUALITY: THE GREAT MORAL ISSUES

Besides teaching and research, the training of leaders is an essential function of the university. The responsibility of the intellectuals, the natural leaders of thought and life, is immense. The anxious preoccupation of the statesmen of all countries at the present moment when competing social, economic and political views are in the field, raises questions of fundamental importance. The issues involved are vital to every interest, both of the individual and of humanity. Universities, which have for their function the conserving and dispensing of the best traditions of human thought and conduct are deeply affected by the great moral issues about the first principles of social organisation, which these questions raise.

Mazzini defined democracy 'as the progress of all through all under the leadership of the wisest and the best.' A democracy fails if the people are not sufficiently enlightened to be able to select wise and intelligent leaders. The leaders today are neither wise nor intelligent. Scepticism and selfishness are their chief characteristics. They are supported by the rapacity of profiteers, the apathy of the masses, the faint-hearted servility of the intellectuals who make themselves the advocates of devastating prejudices which it should be their mission to uproot. Without any clear vision of humanity's goal, our leaders set forth programmes which they value more than the lives of their fellow-men. They will not hesitate to send millions to death to prove themselves in the right. Their own particular purposes should be achieved by any means, however barbarous or inhuman.

We are witnesses today of the terrible and sinister portent that some of the progressive nations of the West whose names are synonymous with advanced civilisation are embarking with cynical deliberation on a course which is in conflict not so much with the high injunctions of the religions they profess, but with the most elementary dictates of natural justice and humanity. In a large part of Europe, democracy which was for long considered the great contribution of Europe to the world's political thought is now abandoned. Parliamentary government is killed, the press is muzzled, freedom of thought, of speech and of assembly is forbidden. The ordinary decencies of public life, the conventions which raise human society above a pack of animals, the bonds of personal loyalty and friendship, are being swept away by groups who neither respect laws nor recognise the common obligations of humanity. The zeal of the dictators shrinks at nothing, not even carefully planned and cold-blooded murders of political opponents.

The obvious incompetence of governments to deal in a just and effective way with the problem of economic inequality is the cause of the discontent with democracy and with this discontent has carried dictators to power. Unimpeded freedom of trade resulted in the exploitation of man by his fellows. The demand for greater economic equality was resented by the vested interests and class conflicts developed. Regulation of private industry on a large scale was undertaken by the governments but not as rapid as one would desire. Economic effort was therefore put under political direction. Peaceful evolution which is the method of democracy yielded to forcible revolution.

Compulsion thus became the controlling principle of social, economic and political life. If there is a restriction of personal liberty and a denial of opportunities for a full, satisfying and noble life, it only means that economic justice and security ask for their price. The price has been paid in many countries, but they are not nearer the goal. The new slavery for mankind has not resulted in economic justice and security.

Selfish and suspicious units which constitute the present politically and economically unorganised world have raised tariff walls which naturally increase personal rivalries and bitterness. It is a state of constant and continuous economic struggle. Those who believe in force for their internal affairs have no hesitation in adopting it in their foreign relations. Militarism is now in the ascendant. Might is today more right than ever. Our dictators are all sabre-rattlers and scaremongers. They tax the sweat and blood of innocent people in order to maintain armaments. Nations are fed on a diet of blood and iron.

When the next war breaks out, we shall have a relapse into barbarism, if not the collapse of civilisation. The world calls itself civilised. Though it has accomplished a good deal in science and organisation, though literature and philosophy, religion and art have been going on for centuries, we find ourselves today as helpless and untutored children in the presence of condition which, if not dealt with and remedied, will bring this civilisation to an end. Mankind has been defined by a cynic as an anthropoid species afflicted with megalomania. Perhaps he is right.

The present crisis is so stupid and yet so serious in its consequences that civilisation itself may be ruined. Mankind must be dragged out of the rut in which it has become wedged and compelled to make a fresh start. A society does not grow out of its own motion. It is carried forward by the efforts of a minority, a 'remnant' in the world of Matthew Arnold, and that minority owes its inspiration to individuals, the wisest and the best, of insight and wisdom, of courage and power. It is the individuals who rise above their national surroundings, who are in communion with the good, seen and unseen, who have the energy to graft their vision on to the existing social substance — it is they who will carry civilisation forward.

Compared with the war-cries and emotional outbursts of the political dictators today, the parting message of Gandhi to the last session of the Indian National Congress is like a ray of heavenly light let into a world of deep darkness: 'I shall never accept self-government brought about by violence.'

Eagerly desirous of India's freedom, foremost among us in his power to further it, he tells us that dear to him as political freedom is, truth and non-violence are yet more dear. He warns his fellow-workers in the Congress to develop a delicate sense of moral responsibility and respect for one's fellow-men which it would be hard to find equalled elsewhere in political struggles. He commands them to transcend the finitude and relativity which belongs to politics as a natural phenomenon and to develop the capacity to apprehend absolute truth and recognise an absolute obligation, all that we include under the names of reason and conscience; truth and love.

As we contemplate the stupendous movement across the pages of history, we witness the power of ideas. Here is a great idea which Gandhi is impressing on the mind and conscience of the people. He appeals to us to rise to new heights, to seek new means of endeavour, to tread new paths towards national reconstruction, greatness and accomplishment, to build a new India on moral and spiritual foundations. In placing the interests of universal truth first and national politics second, he has lit a candle that will not easily be put out. The light of it will have a far penetration in time and in space. It will be seen and welcomed by all honest and sincere people the world over. His appeal will be written not only by the side of the utterances of the great national leaders like Pericles and Cicero, or Washington and Lincoln, but also of great religious reformers, as that of one of the immortal voices of the human race in all that relates to the highest effort of men and nations.

The problem of the great man is an intriguing one, puzzled over by thinkers everywhere in the world. The Chinese democracy of reason answered it in terms offensive to our ears by the dictum that every great man is 'a public calamity'. No wonder there are some who will endorse this dictum with reference to Gandhi, though their number is a steadily diminishing one.

Civilisation is the power to renounce. It is control over selfishness, individual and corporate. It is peaceful co-operation. The tense situation in the world today is the result of the lack of co-operation on terms of justice and equality among the nations of the world. We cannot keep down proud and great peoples either in the West or in the East in perpetual humiliation and bondage and expect peace. Voltaire spoke refreshing candour bordering on cynicism when he said: 'Such is the condition of human affairs that to wish for the greatness of one's country is to wish for the harm of his neighbour.'

When it is said that we get the government we deserve, it means that the State cannot be better than the men who compose it. There is an organic connection between the social conscience and the political arrangement. A more stable and representative government demands a juster social order. A society which tolerates the scourge of untouchability has no right to call itself civilised. There must not be any barrier to the rise of any honest, industrious and capable person to any position for which his character, his intelligence and his talents fit him. Integrity in public life should not be tampered with by caste or communal feeling. The pernicious influences at home and school which inculcate wrong notions about caste superiority and communal contempt require to be removed with a drastic hand. It is no answer to say that each one is at liberty to follow his own customs and creeds but the decencies of social life require, not passive non interference, but active sympathy and understanding.

It is true that we do not shoot or guillotine people, and yet we do things pretty thoroughly in our own way by means of ostracism and social boycott. Hindus and Muslims have lived together for centuries, and yet we cherish the most amazing illusions about each other's characters. By the stubborn cherishing of differences, we develop attitudes which are exploited by the self-seeking and the partisan. 'Are Tories born wicked,' said a child to its Whig mother in the early nineteenth century, 'or do they get wicked as they go on?' 'They are born wicked, my dear, and they get worse.' In our homes, we inoculate young and defenceless children with such poison about each other. Our education, if it is successful should protect us against passion and prejudice, and develop in us a resistance to the power of the press and propaganda to play on our weaknesses.

There can be no social stability without social justice. Democracy is not only political but economic also. Workers must be liberated from grindling toil, poverty and misery so that they may have opportunities for self-development and self-expression. We are certainly more sensitive to the suffering of starving millions and so have developed many philanthropic institutions, sometimes under communal auspices such as orphanages, free boarding for the destitute, hospitals for the sick and the suffering and maternity homes for deserving mothers. All this is excellent so far as it goes, but it is only dealing with the symptoms, not attacking the disease. If mankind cannot achieve something more satisfactory than the present order, our homes and hospitals only prolong our agony, and it is better we starve and stop maternity.

Democratic states, if they are truly representative of the general will, are required to control the productive effort of individuals. The control of natural and economic resources cannot be left to the free play of individual competition. Even private enterprise clamours for state aid to prevent it from collapse. There is not therefore in our century much real opposition to the extension of the public ownership of monopolies except from vested interests. No society can exist without a large measure of social co-operation and control.

But, in no case is it right to surrender our central faith in the power of truth and love to break down resistance to our social endeavours. The social objective is to be gained by persuasion, not force, and it should not involve any suppression of freedom of thought, speech and action, without which human life is deprived of its dignity and value. Social change must be an ordered development and not a violent and disruptive change. For this purpose, enlightened people should support policies which make for public good by educating opinion and propagating right ideas.

We live at a time when history is being re-made. There is unrest in every sphere of life. There are contradictions in aim, confusion of thought in every line. In religion we preach the highest philosophy and are victims of the worst superstition. We quote Plato and Sankara and believe in charms and amulets and offer sacrifices for passing examinations and winning prizes. The growth of national consciousness is retarded by communal separatism. We proclaim the equality for all, but the clash of the caste and the outcaste is growing more and more intense and bitter. Take the economic situation. If anyone visits, say, the city of Calcutta in the Christmas season, and finds out the amount spent on drink and dissipation gambling and betting, he will not consider the people of the place to be any means poor and yet the existence of the slums and those who live in them under conditions hardly to be borne are a sad commentary on the utter economic chaos and injustice.

The mass of poverty, the extent of illiteracy, the social obstacles in the way of improvement, the tangled undergrowth of vested interests, religious, political and economic, reveal not one problem but an infinity of problems. Many of us have an emotional apprehension of the vastness and complexity of the situation, but what is required is a scientific view. There are no short cuts to their solution. Here is work for a number of university men and women, to disentangle the confused issues, to reconcile the conflicting aims, to melt the various influences for good into one supreme social effort which is essential to make men less selfish, less aggressive, less given to frivolity. It is for the universities to produce men who are able to stand out of the welter of commonplace egoism and seek the public good, who have intellectual conscience to see the truth and the moral courage to pursue it. Man is not on earth to be happy. He is here to be honest, to be decent, to be good. Whether you get a prize post or not, it is open to you to be useful to your fellows and to work for truth, not because you hope to win but because your cause is just.

True liberty does not lie in the individual's independence of social control. It consists rather in the deliberate regulation of social forces for the positive development of the individual.

CHAPTER 7

LIBERTY AND FREEDOM: PERSONAL AND SOCIAL

The chief function of a university, to my mind, is to give training in that greatest of all arts, the art of living together. In these troubled times when the outlook is wilder and danger more visible, it is also the most difficult of all arts. Society is in a state of upheaval. For the down and out, for the hungry and the homeless, all talk about political liberty and cultural freedom is a mockery. I do not wish to dogmatise on the exact nature of our trouble, but may it not be some fundamental flaw in the very constitution of organised society, something anarchical in the relation of men to one another?

There is much sympathy for the deaf and the dumb, for the blind and the lame, but little for the poor and the unemployed, though the latter far exceed the former in numbers. We complain of the indifference of Nature, but acquiescence in the inhumanity of man. We demand of Nature an equity she does not possess, but are loathe to practise it ourselves.

The constitution for India imposes safeguards on the exercise of political power so as to eliminate its capricious and irresponsible use. The need for safeguards is perhaps greater in the economic field. In our present social context economic liberty can be secured only by surrounding economic power with safeguards in order that the essential material conditions of a civilised life may be brought within the reach of all. True liberty does not lie in the individual's independence of social control. It consists rather in the deliberate regulation of social forces for the positive development of the individuals who constitute society. It is not a question of a compromise between the freedom of the individual and the necessity for social action. A new sense of social wholeness alone can stem the rot in our present condition.

This does not mean that we must take to the forms of political mysticism which requires us to surrender ourselves, body and soul, to the State. There are countries today which have made society into a prison built on the ruins of liberty. In many parts of the world, the state of liberty reminds one of the remarks which a shrewd Frenchman made on being shown the Statue of Liberty from the New York harbour; 'We too have monuments to our departed.' In the new slavery which is becoming fashionable, the individual is denied the elementary right of freedom of thought and speech. The test of a social order is the quality of the persons whom it nourishes and the extent to which it elicits the creative energies of individuals. The economic order must be so revised as to permit rather than crush the development of individual responsibility. A true society cannot be built out of slaves, but only out of free, self-respecting, educated men and women.

Even as a decent social order cannot be built out of slaves, a world commonwealth cannot be composed of slave nations.

As social freedom and equality are the basis of the State, so is international freedom the essential condition of a peaceful world order. The organic commonwealth of free peoples, which is the only foundation of liberty and peace, is still a vision, but a vision which has inspired great minds and great efforts, that will continue to inspire the renewal of those efforts in years to come.

University training today is not a mere invitation to pleasant intellectual speculation. It is a summon to action, a summon to be and become different, to know the fatal consequences of muddle-headedness, timidity, inertia, and overcome them. It must endow us with a vision for equality and brotherhood, political, economic and social, and charge us with a passion for realising it. Great ideas can be achieved only by great means. The method of democracy substitutes reason and persuasion for force and compulsion. It consists in the development of understanding and co-operation, in the agreement to reach decisions by discussion and consent. By the right employment of democratic institutions, radical changes in the existing order can be brought about without bloodshed and revolution. Democracy can save itself only by becoming aristocratic. Its leaders must be men of integrity and independence, of discernment and devotion to truth. It becomes mob rule if astute and unscrupulous politicians inflame the mob and direct it to their own selfish ends. Democracy assumes that the common individual is wise enough to know his own interests and good enough to wish them for others. Relatively few even among the so-called educated are able to think for themselves without submitting their minds to external control and vested interests. It is therefore essential that the leaders are wisely and carefully chosen.

When once the policies are laid down by the democratic bodies, their execution must be left to experts. All government is skilled work. To allow the people to run the government in any other sense would be like allowing the pupils to run a school or the passengers to run a train.

Graduates of Indian universities will be soon called upon to occupy positions of skill and responsibility. In the classroom and the debating society, in the hostel and the playground, through the play of mind on mind, through freedom of thought and speech, they must be educated to think honestly, tolerantly and lovingly, to discern the good and choose the best. It is in the university that we must learn to develop the free mind, to cultivate charity of outlook, to strive to understand points of view other than our own. 'I have laboured carefully,' says Spinoza, 'not to mock, lament or execrate, but to *understand* human actions.' To understand and look upon events and ideas, without the loss of self-command, without the intolerance of the fanatic, is what we expect from university men.

The condition of our country today, with its social abuses, with its communal feuds, with its poverty and unemployment along with the increased control over the direction of affairs, political and economic, will give ample scope and opportunity to our young men of vision, courage and self-sacrifice. In the service of their country, in their endeavour to establish social justice, clean politics and right relations between men and women, they will find perfect freedom. In all their efforts I hope they will bear in mind the simple truth that patience in the face of failure will not endanger our cause, but impatience may.

If the rule of reason in the region of thought is the aim of science, the rule of equality in the region of behaviour is the aim of democracy.

CHAPTER 8

INTELLECTUAL INTEGRITY

It was a hundred years ago that Macaulay produced his famous document. In pursuance of that document, on March 7, 1835, Lord William Bentinck, the then Governor-General, issued the historic resolution in which it was laid down that 'the great object of the British government ought to be the promotion of European literature and science among the natives of India.' The introduction of western education has quickened our national life and activities. There are criticisms, just and legitimate, that the system of education introduced into this country by the East India Company when they set apart a lakh of rupees for the education of the people of India, was not a comprehensive one. The education imparted was of a literary and theoretical character, designed to train clerks for the routine work of the bureaucratic administration and not to train leaders for a democratic state. Primary education has been woefully neglected.

The villagers, who constitute the bulk of India's population, live in an environment which has remained unchanged for centuries. If anything, conditions have grown worse.

As communications developed and railways penetrated the interior, the village craftsman, the potter, the weaver and the blacksmith, were obliged to give up their hereditary professions and seek a bare subsistence from the soil. Crude and medieval methods of agriculture are still being applied. Higher scientific and technical education has never been thought of. We cannot lay the blame on the rulers, for even in European countries, elementary education is only a recent achievement. For a long time almost all who were educated were trained in Latin and Greek, grammar, logic and rhetoric. Outlook and control are changing, and I have no doubt that the Central Advisory Board of Education will do something to reorient our policy in education and insist on the spread of elementary education as well as higher scientific and technical education.

I am concerned now not so much with the details of the Western system of education as with its general character and spirit. Two essential features leap to one's eyes, the scientific spirit and the democratic method. I do not propose to deal here with the contributions to scholarship and science made by the intellectuals of our country. The old conception that college men live a life of their own and devote themselves exclusively to study and research, to thought and discussion, has now changed. The function of a college is to produce not only men of high learning and scholarship but also those best fitted and trained for leadership of the community. I must warn my young friends that study and training are different from participation in the struggle. It is ruinous to their interests if they allow themselves to be carried away by their emotions and stampeded into immature political action in the precious years when they are to prepare themselves for the struggle of life.

The superiority of the West is due to its intellectual integrity, the sincerity of its pursuit of truth. From the time of Socrates, the seeker of truth, down till today, the Western mind, with rare exceptions, has been remarkably free from self-complacency, intellectual laziness and blind faith in ancient wisdom. It has never lost the sense of wonder, the eager curiosity to know and find out for oneself by observation and experiment, the truth of the near and the far. Science had made life easier for millions of men and women. Our educators tried to impart to us the scientific mind. The possession of the scientific spirit is not the same as the capacity to use scientific devices. We may be able to use the telephone and the wireless, the railways and the aeroplane, and yet be lacking in the scientific mind which is something organic and structural and not merely outward and decorative. The scientific spirit must be applied not only to the ordinary arrangement of life and leisure, to the distribution of the material goods, to the improvement of industry and agriculture, but also to the things which touch the mind and the morals of the community.

Our scientific conscience must be shocked not only by the contrasts of fabulous wealth and grovelling poverty but also by those of intense holiness and diseased superstition. In our relations with one another, we have failed to apply scientific and social wisdom. This failure is writ large on our society. Social abuses like untouchability are tolerated simply because the spirit in us is suppressed by the force of custom. They are practised by otherwise kindly people who have ceased to feel and whose understanding is petrified by tradition. There are millions in our country today who use scientific devices and yet revere superstition as mystical revelation and adhere to absurd social customs in the name of tradition. In this matter there is no real conflict between science and religion. The Supreme does not tell us: 'I am tradition', but only 'I am Truth'. We owe reverence to the seekers of truth, who conquer our minds by the spirit of truth, and not to the conformists, who enslave our minds in the name of tradition. Tradition cannot ever supersede truth. What is manifestly wrong cannot become right by the mere force of custom or authority. Conscience cannot be silenced by scripture. We must clear our mind of the cowebs which are found there.

There are some in our country who use scientific facts and theories to buttress their own pet prejudices. They argue that mill was anticipated by Manu and aeroplanes were found in ancient India. They quote the latest researches of anthropologists and eugenists to defend the cruelties of caste. When passion and prejudice clothe themselves in the garb of scientific respectability, when they invent a pseudoscience to save themselves from true science, they become most dangerous. We must develop a scientific conscience, an intellectual sobriety and view matters involving passionate emotions with dispassion. We must help the common people to build convictions which mob psychology and mass hysteria cannot touch. Young men trained in our colleges are called upon to engage in the crusade of intelligence against superstition in the hope that the truth shall make us free. Truth and freedom are one and the same and if our colleges and universities abandon the search for truth and the pursuit of freedom, if they fail to enrich the spirit of man in its best aspirations, they will become utterly soulless.

If the rule of reason in the region of thought is the aim of science, the rule of equality in the region of behaviour is the aim of democracy. Democracy is not a political arrangement or a form of government. It is a pattern of life, an active conviction which informs and inspires every thought, word and deed. Our present constitution of society induces in its more fortunate members far too great readiness to accept privilege as though it were inherent in the social order, as though it were normal and even proper and just. If we are sincere in our professions of democracy, we should not shut our eyes to the most obvious defects of the present social order. A system which does not offer security and decent employment to multitudes of trained young men suffers from some fundamental vice. Society is in danger of splitting to pieces if the few who have the benefits of civilisation are not willing to share them with the rest.

No State is stable unless it procures for all its members the essentials of a good life. We acknowledge that health is better than disease, sufficiency better than poverty, shelter better than cold and exposure; ease of mind better than racking anxiety. It is our duty to obtain these essentials of civilised life for the mass of the population, to work for basic economic justice for all, if necessary by the imposition of higher taxes on incomes, land values and inheritance. Riches were created by the maker for being spent on social purpose. *Yajnaya srstani dhanani dhatra* (*Mahabharata*). It was Blackstone, not Lenin, who wrote:

> 'The law not only regards life and protects every man in the enjoyment of it but also furnishes him with everything necessary for its support. For there is no man so indigent or wretched but that he may demand a supply sufficient for all the necessities of life from the more opulent part of the community.'

There are basic industries for which the State offers bounties and there is no strong reason why their management should not be undertaken by the State itself. It will ensure the employment of Indians in the higher ranks as well as efficiency of management. If the instruments of production are owned by the community, the present owners may be paid reasonable compensation for their displacement. A revision of the land revenue system is urgently called for. While a democrat has nothing in common with the extremist who stands for free love, atheism and the dividing up of property all round, he has every sympathy for a peaceful attainment of a more equitable social order. But these ends must be attained by the method of democracy, which substitutes persuasion for force. The end is not to be reached by fierce revolutionary struggle. The method of democracy is opposed to the intolerance and bigotry which once upon a time beat men to death for religious heresies, and today in many parts of the world adopt the same drastic method in regard to unpalatable political opinions.

In our country today, there are forces which are working against democracy. Religious labels possess political significance. Young men grow up in surroundings which encourage sectarian and communal prejudice. From their early days; they are trained to look upon clannishness and communalism as normal conditions of life. Petty local feelings are everywhere on the increase. A vulgar rampancy of provincial feeling is not known to be an offence against patriotism and humanity. Even those who pose as nationalists have an exalted idea of their duty to their own community and a crude sense of their duty to their fellow-men. Naturally corruption and nepotism prevail in high places. In a competitive world, the country must have the services of the best brains at its command. Every sincere democrat will strive hard to free the country from the bondage to communalism and slavery to sects. We must educate men for citizenship not in a Nazi or a Fascist State but in a liberal, democratic State.

Scientific outlook and social idealism are transforming our political ambitions. If we press for self-government, it is not because we wish to see a few of our countrymen in high places, but because we desire to secure a decent life for the masses. If we wish to shake off political subjection, it is to end the suffering of our countrymen. Nationalist sentiment today is not confined to the intellectuals or the politically minded classes. This great change is due to one personality.

From time to time, in this imperfect world, appear rare souls endowed with genius, who have the capacity to find out what is wrong, the ability to guide their generation, the courage to confront adverse forces, and the faith to lead their nation to victory. Gandhi is one such. He was the first to point out that our political condition is not to be regarded in isolation. It is just the symptom of a disease from which the whole body politic is suffering. The affliction that is visited on us is the return for our common failure. We must give up the self-satisfied and unworthy air of injured innocence. Our offences with regard to women and the low castes have been grave and we must submit to a heavy penance.

Those who look upon our political slavery as the external violence of a band of robbers preying on innocent people have a very narrow conception of history. The historic destinies of people cannot be dismissed so lightly. The British are not brigands who have fallen on India in the highway of her history and bound her hand and foot. British rule is a much deeper phenomenon, reflecting the serious organic defects of Indian society. It is the outward symptom of an inward crisis, of loss of faith, of hideous weakening of our moral life, our indiscipline and disunion, our violence and vulgarity. To use Robert Bridges' phrase, it is our 'crowed uncleaness of soul' that is responsible for our backward condition. This requires to be overcome. We cannot build a new India unless we first rebuild ourselves. The immediate task confronting us is moral purgation, spiritual regeneration. It alone can bring national rebirth and freedom.

The last fifty years have seen a notable advance in the general life of our country. It is true that we are living in a world of communal jealousies, growing inter-provincial ill-feeling, the miseries of unemployment, the anxiety that comes from economic insecurity and competitive pressure and wilful omission of opportunities for happiness. Not to be disturbed by these would require a cynicism or a dullness of comprehension that happily are rare. But there is no need to lose heart. While I am sensible of the dangers that surround us, I see no sign whatever of the decadence of the essential values of life, and judged by ordinary standards the advance that we have made is singularly great and rapid. During the past fifty years a social revolution has taken place in our country as elsewhere, far more basic in its effects than anything we have had in the past. Because it operates without external violence, many fail to realise that it is a revolution at all. The most striking manifestation of this change is to be seen among the young.

While it is dangerous to draw general conclusions from one's own limited experience, I shall hazard the observation that present day students have on the whole more seriousness of purpose, more public spirit and sense of human brotherhood, and in the mass of the people there is certainly a great advance in education and above all in the desire for education. I know that there are dangers lurking in the new freedom but they are not comparable to those attending the old enslavement. If some of us are shocked by the follies and pretensions of eager youth, who believe that vigorous action is admirable even when it is misguided, let us put them down for the extravagance of the new ideal of the fulfilment of democracy and economic justice.

I know the age has become vulgar. Tests and the sense for tradition which we associated with cultivated men are on the decrease. The bad manners of the emancipated, the general tendency to connive at shady transactions, if they seem to bring in success and popularity, the bad taste shown even by well-bred people in times of excitement and elections, the absence of restraint in daily discussions, sometimes make one despair whether democracy is worth fighting for. But let us not judge it by its present phase. The educated men are the natural leaders of the community. They lead the conscience of the country. If only they are endowed with the true vision of spirit, which engenders the democratic feeling in social, economic and political affairs, if they participate in the struggle in a spirit of service and dedication and not with motives of lust for power and profit, they will expedite our national progress. Do nothing which will bring discredit to your cause or dishonour to your country.

The honour of the motherland is a sacred trust. I may conclude with Bernard Shaw's words: 'This is the true joy in life, the being used for a purpose recognised by yourself as a mighty one; the being thoroughly worn out before you are thrown on the scrap heap; the being a force of nature, instead of a feverish, selfish, little clod of ailments and grievances, complaining that the world will not devote itself to making you happy.'

There is such a thing as the logic of history. If we are where we are, it is because we are what we are.

CHAPTER 9

INTELLECTUAL CONSCIENCE

The responsibility of the intellectuals of a country is great. If we want to know the opinion of a nation on any important question, we do not consult its men-servants and maid-servants. It is the leaders of a country that represent its public sentiments and aspirations and mould them. The history of the world tells us that slavery and serfdom were not abolished by the collective will of the slaves and the serfs.

Democracy, so long as it is what it is, imperfectly educated, throws a great responsibility on the leaders. The average voter even in educated England has no opinion of his own on many questions. He chooses his party by tradition or by his agreement with its central aims in those matters on which he has strong views. On other questions he takes his opinions from his leaders. His conscience is clear when the party is chosen and for the rest the leaders decide and the voters obey. If on the 3rd August,

1914, Sir Edward Grey had declared for neutrality, most Liberals would have accepted it as the soundest policy; as he happened to declare for intervention, that was considered quite the right thing. In a complex social machine, it is difficult for the units to exercise thought. It is more easy to be obedient automata. It does not even pay to think. Perhaps, thought may prove costly. If the leaders want to create public opinion, the machinery of the press and the wireless makes it most easy.

Modern conditions afford propagandists vastly increased opportunities of promoting collective excitement and setting the world in a conflagration. A few clever and adventurous leaders can excite people's passions and suppress intellectual freedom. In these circumstances, truth does not win—there is no attempt to find out truth; we prove that what we do desire is truth. It becomes very plausible if we introduce facts and figures. They give a semblance of truth and objectivity. We can be objective and yet untruthful. We may make a show of logic and yet be partisan. Such is the nature of what is called propaganda, which is responsible for all the great disasters of the world.

When you, young men and women, enter your life careers, bar or journalism, commerce or industry, the service of the State or the profession of teaching, you will be the chief agents in the guidance of opinion. You will take a large share in the creation and maintenance of high levels of public opinion and duty. It depends on you whether you are going to be propagandists or prophets of the ideal. In the difficult days ahead of us, only those who neither organise propaganda nor fall victims to it can be helpful.

I am not a politician, but only a student, an observer from the outside. As a teacher of some years' standing, who has worked in different parts of India, I may claim to know the mind of the youth of the country. The situation has an appeal for students of psychology, and an urgency for those interested in the healing of nations. India today is in the throes of a Renaissance. There is a realisation that the nations which are bound by tradition over much do not make any progress. The civilisation of the ancient Hindus and the Greeks developed in an atmosphere of freedom. When the human mind is enslaved by tyranny of any kind, social or economic, political or religious, we have a Dark Age.

It is no accident that the great progress in knowledge and scientific activity in modern Europe coincides exactly with the centuries which have marked as loosening of the grip of authority on the mind of man. A recognition of this fact is in the main responsible for the revolt against authority which is expressing itself in the movements for freedom in religious, social, economic and political fields. When the dust and din of present controversies are over, it would be put down to the lasting credit of Great Britain that she roused the sense of pride and self-respect of a great people and made them keenly conscious of the shame of subjection. At a time of life when impressions are freely received and assimilated, when the world has brought no disappointment to love or frustration to endeavour, when the appeal of idealism is intense and the gates of the future seem wide open, young men and women read the history of freedom-movements. You do not expect them to read the story of Thermophlae without any emotion. You do not expect them to construe the march of Garibaldi from Palermo to Naples as an exercise in walking along the Serpentine. The adventures of the European nations are not studied solely from the point of view of the final examination. They thrill imagination and kindle aspiration.

It is not a matter for surprise that our young men, trained in the history of Western nations and taught for years that nothing is more precious than freedom, that freedom is not only necessary but more essential than anything else in life, have learnt the lesson and are now repeating it. Without freedom, one's country is only a prison. Let us have an India poor and free, rather than rich and in bondage. That is what we hear. When our young men come out to foreign countries and find that the Chinese, the Japanese, the Czech and the Turk are citizens of free countries, while the best of them have to bend their heads in shame, it is no wonder that some of them feel the situation so bitterly that they shrink at nothing.

I have no doubt that no true Britishers would wish to see India pledge herself to the support of British control in perpetuity; nor is there an Indian who will sever the British connection if it earns its right to be preserved. The cry for independence is the cry of despair. If what the propagandist press asserts is true, that after one hundred and fifty years of British rule the country would lapse into anarchy and drift into disaster if the British should withdraw, if that is true, it is argued, there can be no more complete indictment of British rule and justification for independence. If helplessness is the price India has to pay for the continuance of British rule, it is our duty to resist and repel it at any cost. These panicky statements need not be taken at their face value. If the cry goes forth from Great Britain 'let us govern', the response comes from India 'let us cut away.' If the Rothermere Press says that independence would mean anarchy and bloodshed, the non-cooperator replies, 'Better go to hell than suffer slavery on earth.' 'To be eaten up by the hordes from Northern most and Central Asia' would be 'a position infinitely superior to one of ever growing emasculation.'

It is a vicious circle that is operating. The Britisher is anxious to quell the qualms of an uneasy conscience by talking in season and out of season of the intellectual inferiority of the Indian, his impractical loyalties, social abuses, illiteracy, ignorance, etc.,

etc. These are set forth as a justification of the British rule. But everyone of these provokes the resentment of the Indian and stirs him to the very depths. The very grounds which the Britisher is anxious to repeat in self-justification cause bitterness in the Indian heart. If the process goes on of British contempt for the Indian and the Indian's distrust of the British, things are bound to come to a head. If two groups of men move in such an atmosphere, of condescension and contempt, patronage and pity on the one side and suspicion and distrust, hatred and bitterness on the other, we are preparing for a first class crisis, if not a deadly conflict. Indo-British friendship, which is the greatest world issue today, will be a great step towards the peace of the world, and it is an ideal great enough to make us take risks for it, without talking of dumb masses, humbugs and half-wits.

Friends of peace in India have now a great opportunity of working for the larger objective and binding India to Britain. Such a partnership would help to terminate the age-long conflict of East and West and be of lasting benefit to the human race. If a political system could contain two great sections of mankind, one European and the other Asiatic, on a footing of justice and equality and in a community of spirit, it will prepare for the world federation. It requires nothing more than goodwill and sympathy. Are they difficult to get? Lord Haldance some time before his death wrote in a letter to me: 'We Britishers are lacking in imagination and so fail in sympathy.' Theoretical justice, practical common sense, a perception of the realities of the case and world peace demand Indian freedom and it is the duty of the clear-sighted and the forward-looking to foster it.

To my Indian friends, I would say, worthy ambitions are not enough, worthy techniques are also necessary. Ideas are poor things until we equip them with wings. The way in which the resolution of independence was passed by men qualifying for the Bar or preparing for the Civil Service, shows the levity and light-heartedness with which serious matters are described and dealt with. The world is not in the hands of blind inconsequence. There is such a thing as the logic of history. If we are where we are, it is because we are what we are. We do no service to our country if we pretend that difficulties do not exist. It is no use imagining that there is nothing wrong with ourselves and all that is necessary is a change of government and the millennium would flower in our backgarden the next morning. We would not be able to wipe off our ignorance and misery, our poverty and unemployment.

If we want to win the rubber of life, to use a metaphor from the game of Bridge, we have to discard our weak suits and develop our strong ones. Self-government cannot be talked into existence. There is a good deal of work to be done on the home front in social and economic matters. A silent revolution is taking place in the structure of our society. The old bonds are breaking down and a new integration of forms is taking place. There is a slow but steady shifting of the population from the villages to towns. The political and social emancipation of women has not had its full effects worked out. We cannot reopen a past page of history and we require an increased alliance of science and social organisation. It is not the part of courage to abandon difficult problems to Providence. By the conscious and deliberate application of human intelligence, they could and must be solved.

Of course we must understand what elements have entered into the national psychology, what the subliminal consciousness of a community contains. The physical weakness, the degenerate manhood of the country is the direct result of social practices. The physical weakness of the people is due to improper diet and lack of sanitation. Clear thinking on many of these problems is necessary. Mere agitation won't carry us far. It is your duty to plan and to build. When you go back and find a thousand things waiting to be done, what will you do—join the race for wealth, scramble for place and power and forsake your ideals of today? I ask that question because I know men who were honest and sincere and thoroughly courageous in their university days bade goodbye to all that when they got into the Indian atmosphere. The atmosphere is an acid test. Not many are able to stand it. Will you be of that large number who dreamed great dreams in their university days and became hardened cynics in after life? Let each one answer for himself. India wants every one of you to stand up against the disruptive agencies of caste and creed and make her more glorious than ever.

Social reconstruction will follow if you undertake the less exciting but more exalting task of individual remaking.

CHAPTER 10

THE TEST OF CIVILISED LIFE

It heartens one to see that at least in our women's conference the distinctions of high and low, Hindu and Muslim, European and Indian, official and non-official, are not observed. By their very nature, these conferences constitute a rebuke and a challenge to men, and I do hope that your lesson will not be lost on us. It is a matter of sincere pleasure to all patriots that you are up against communalism in every sense of the term, and we hope that you will persist in fighting it.

The conference modestly declares that it is interested only in the field of educational and social reform. You need not be afraid that you are dealing only with secondary issues, simply because political objectives are not put in the front of your programme. You are also contributing in a very direct way to the political emancipation of this country. The extent of our political backwardness and failure is directly proportioned to the strength of our social and communal differences and appalling illiteracy: and if you attack these, you will assist our progress towards the political goal. We cannot achieve political freedom, we cannot maintain it for long even if we achieve it, unless these social and communal difficulties are removed.

Again, what is the good of achieving political freedom if thereby we are not able to produce a fine civilisation? Science and politics may give us security of life, food, shelter and freedom from disorder, but these are transitory trifles compared with those central situations of life, like love and motherhood, and such personal relationships, and the test of civilised life lies in the strength and equanimity with which we are able to face these deeper realities as against the mere frills of life.

I agree that it is essential to liberate men and women from the external tyranny to which they are now being subjected. It is necessary that the crude views which persist in treating women as domestic servants or social ornaments or sexual conveniences should be put an end to. But it is only one part of the task, the negative; the positive work lies in the development of the personal resources. If we neglect the latter task, we do so at our peril.

Look at what is happening today in countries where this negative emancipation from outward bondage has been achieved without sufficient emphasis, on the positive. People are freed from the fear of religion, the fear of the priest, the fear of hell, the fear of the policeman, and yet they are becoming world-weary at twenty-two. They have attained liberty but it has turned out a Dead Sea fruit. The emancipated women may enjoy rank, wealth, position, may even knowledge; they may know French and play on the organ, but what then? They do not know what to do with themselves. They rush here and there among outward things, pushing, carrying, dragging, busy tying this knot and untying the other, blaming this person and cursing another; they sulk, they sneer, they scold, and complain bitterly against all and sundry that the elements are unfriendly and they are not having a nice time. They waste their emotions on vulgar inanities, and the frippery and the tinsel absorb all their energies. When they escape into solitude, they have a strained, harassed, hunted, nervous look. A nameless sadness weighs them down and they become delirious and deranged when the shocks and the outrages of life overtake them. Life has become what we see in pictures and cinemas, an idiot's tale full of pain and piffle, signifying nothing. It has no living sense or purpose. Liberty from external restrictions is not enough.

A state of things in which everybody is free to do what he likes, read what he likes, is infinitely more dangerous than one in which everybody is kept in bondage by social codes and ecclesiastical pandits. To liberate individuals from the bonds laid on them by external authority is good and necessary; to liberate them from the servitude which is infinitely more perilous and degrading, the servitude to one's own passions and desires, is equally necessary and urgent.

With all humility and due respect, may I urge that only those who are genuine and profound can serve society. This sincerity and strength one cannot get by easy living and light sentiment. A new social order cannot be created solely by means of scientific devices or humanitarian goodwill. The great majority of altruistic minded people acquire a sense of satisfaction that they are doing their bit, when they enrol themselves as members of social reform associations or fellowship organisations or subscribe to their funds. It is all splendid work, and far be it from me to minimise its value.

But what is it when compared to that more important task of deepening one's own life and making it worth while. Only such deepened spirits can assist human beings to bear the anguish they are called upon to endure and not the mere professional reformers or physicians of the soul, to whom all griefs and sorrows are of one type. The poor are not confined to the slums, nor the so-called fallen to the streets. There are helpless human souls in crowded offices, in stuffy drawing rooms, in desolate bedrooms where they toss about restlessly, eating their hearts out, and if we have to know of their constant efforts and strivings, we have to approach them as human souls, not as social uplifters, by making them feel that they are not sadly and insupportably alone. To give the lowly and the lost sympathy and understanding is to wash their sores and clean their stains.

A human soul reveals itself to another only in love and sympathy, and not in answer to questionnaires and in mental clinics. It yearns for warm love and is repelled by cold curiosity. Go through a day with calm and serenity and understand the hearts of men and women you meet with, and look on the world with their eyes, and you will do more for society than by working at office desks or distributing pamphlets at public meetings or going about with a little notebook and a bit of pencil. Social reconstruction will follow if you undertake the less exciting but more exacting task of individual remaking.

When you emphasise the inner, the deeper spiritual side of religion, they unite the world.

CHAPTER 11

THE TRUE SPIRIT OF RELIGION

The one fact of our age is the confrontation of different cultures and different religions. Once upon a time we used to have religions working in parallel lines without much influence on one another. Today we are thrown together. The world has become a physical unity. There is nearness and neighbourhood. But it should also become an integrated entity.

How have religions been functioning? When you emphasise the formal aspects of religions, they divide the world. When you emphasise the inner, the deeper spiritual side of religion, they unite the world. We must try to find out what the real significance of religion is. The religious quest is not something which is supererogatory. Every human individual has the craving to find out what this world consists of. Is this cosmic panorama all? Or is there a constant presence behind, informing, animating and giving life to this whole cosmic process? It is the question which we raise. Every thoughtful person has raised it. The *Gitā* says, *anityam asukham lokam.* The *Upanīsad* writer tells us: this world is *asat,* unreal; this world is *mṛtyu,* death; this world is *tamas,* darkness. Is there a way out? That is the question which he asks.

The Buddha, when he saw the signs of old age, sickness and death, asked, 'Is this all, or is there anything we can get from out of this succession of mundane states?' He met a yogi who said: 'Oh! best of men! Afraid of this life of birth and death, I have given up this world. For what? For liberating myself from this circuit of *saṁsāra.* I am struggling to find whether there is anything eternal, anything which breathes on the temporal or whether these successions of stages leading to annihilation are all.' But simply because we ask for something, it does not follow that, that something has a reality. I may ask for food but food may not be there.

You may ask whether there is anything which exists behind the panorama; but simply because you ask for it does not follow that it is there. So we try, as reasonable beings, to find out by reason, by logical reflection whether there is anything. The answer we give is, 'Try, look at the world, look at the experience, look at how things happen.' From matter we go to life; from life we go to *manas,* mind; from *manas* we go to *jñāna,* intelligence; from intelligence we rise to *ānanda,* Absolute Reality, freedom. The cosmic process is a staircase, so to say, leading from one stage to another.

By means of logical reflection we assert that there is some reality, something which serves as the basis of all. But intellectual speculation is different from spiritual realization. We cannot be satisfied with logical inference. There is a difference between saying, 'There is God', and feeling the reality of God in our nature; *anubhavāvasānameva vidyā phalam.* The fruit of knowledge, the fruit of *vidyā* is *anubhava.* So we say no man can be regarded as truly fulfilled unless he is able to rise from the discords, doubts and difficulties of intellect and gets himself illumined, rises to a higher state of consciousness; when he gets pure tranquillity of spirit; when he is able to say, 'I have known the truth.'

If, therefore, we raise the question whether there is anything, we infer logically that there should be something, and we see face to face. This seeing face to face requires a churning of our mind, a discipline of our whole being. We must be transformed in our nature. We must be different from what we are. That is the meaning of attaining *anubhava* or illumination. It is the man who has so changed himself that he can say he has seen the Reality — not others. 'Blessed are the pure in heart for they shall see God.' Seeing of God is a consequence of purity of heart. We must pass through severe intellectual discipline. We must change ourselves so completely that we can say, 'I have seen the Supreme. In my life-time, in my flesh, I have seen the Ultimate Reality.'

But people with *anubhava* have given different account of Reality. Which are we to accept? *Kanāda* says one thing, Jaimini says another thing. What is it that we have to take for granted? Our scriptures have been emphatic, from the beginning, that there must be hospitality so far as the treatment of the Supreme and of the prayers we address to Him are concerned. If we are able to say that, then we will see that the descriptions which are given — halting, imperfect as they are—they ought not to be made to conflict with each other. There is a harmony, *samanvaya* reconciliation of all these things. We call him Siva, we call him Viṣṇu, we call him the Buddha, we call him by any name; but the metaphysical reality is one and the same.

We know the verse which says: I am a Saivite. I chant the *paari mantra (oṁnamaḥ śivāya)* but my heart turns to the darling of the *Gopis*.

janārdano vā maheśvaro vā
na vastu-pratipattir asti

Whether you call it Janardana or Maheśvara, there is no distinction in reality. These are names, but all roads lead to the same God, the same Supreme, and we should not quarrel about names we give to it.

The question, the logical answer, the intuitive illumination and a spirit of harmony among the descriptions, etc., which we have, this is nothing dogmatic, nothing sectarian, nothing peculiar to this or that; it is something which has come down to us from the beginning of our history. We find there: *tad viṣṇoḥ paramaṁ padam sadā paśyanti sūrayaḥ paśyanti* is the word used. We see the divine nature, where it dwells and then the way in which we describe it:

esa devo viśvakarmā ṃahātmā
sadā janānām hrdave sannivistah
hrdā manias manasābhiklipto
ya enaṁ viduramṛtās te bhavanti

Through understanding, will and imagination, we fabricate that reality into the idiom which suits us. So it will have different forms.

It will not have this particular form or that Samkarācārya tells us:

sa ca bhaguvā jñānaiśvarya śaktibalavirya tejobhih,
sadā sampannaḥ, triguṇātmikā visnaviṁ svām māyām
mūlaprakṛtim vaśikṛtya, ajo avyayo bhutānām iśvaro
nityaśuddhabuddhamnkta-svabhāv opi san svamāyayā
dehavān iva jāta iva, lokānugrahaṁ lokānugrahaṁ
kurvanniva laksyate.

That one Supreme assumes different forms to oblige suffering humanity.

He comes in the form of the Buddha, Mahavira, Nanak, or any of the great teachers. They are all messengers of the Supreme Light and the messengers may not always agree with one another but the harmony of all descriptions is the essential fact of our religion. So far as these spiritual aspects are concerned, so far as these personal experiences are concerned, we listen to what people have to say, *sravaṛa;* we think about what they say, *manana;* we make it part of our being, it becomes *ātma darśana.* It is equated with the insight into the Supreme itself.

Similarly, the *Gita* tells us *tad viddhi raṇipātena paripraśnena sevayā praṇipāta,* is listening to a teacher, prostrating ourselves; *paripraśna* is cross-examining him, asking him all questions. *Seva,* by service to him we assimilate the truth, make it a part of our very being. We become different. Human fulfilment is the answer to man's question. He is not really a realised soul if he merely repeats texts, discusses philosophy. It is a prophetic soul, it is the man who has experienced it, who is the true individual. Priestly religion is one thing; the philosophical religion is another; the prophetic religion is the highest. It is there that the individual himself becomes a messenger of Light.

While these things are accepted throughout the world as forming the basic background of India's thought, we have not adhered to it systematically. We have diverted ourselves, we have gone away from the true path. We think by doing this or doing that we are likely to attain salvation. That is a wrong thing. About the caste system, for example, *Vedanta Desika* says:

śvapaco'pi mahipāla viṣṇnbhakto dvijādhikaḥ
viṣṇu bhakti vihí naśca yatiś ca svapacādhamaḥ

If we do not have that spirit in us, if we have not got love of God, if we have not got the sense of spiritual values; it is not a question whether we are born this way or that way; even if we are dog-eaters, if we have got love of God, we are the highest of all; if we do not have it; then we are lower than the lowest.

In other words, what caste we belong to, to what condition we belong, is a matter of our character, the way in which we behave.

vrksañ chitvā paśūn hatvā kṛtvā rudhira-kardamam
yady evam gamyate svargam narakam kena gamyate

If by cutting trees, killing animals, making blood flow, we attain salvation, what is the way to hell, the critic asks.

In other words, we are doing things which are exactly opposed to the fundamental preachings of our religion. We do them and if our people are condemned and criticized, if they do not get on well in other countries, it is because they are not the representatives of the spiritual culture of our country. They are the representatives of the traditional dogmas and usages.

Let us understand in what the essence of our culture consists, what in Hindu *Dharma,* and that we should not practise things which are really opposed to Hindu *Dharma.* Every day we do them. We believe in God, but do things which betray our adherence to the world, the flesh and the devil. Anyone who believes in God will not adopt attitudes which we sometimes adopt. We have to scrutinize ourselves, examine ourselves, ask ourselves every day a question, whether we are true believers of God or merely counterfeit believers. That is what we have to understand.

I do hope that if our religion rids itself of these pernicious practices which in the growth of centuries have come about, it will be able to consolidate this world, it will be able to tell people that there is a religion which has allowed peaceful friendly co-operation among all. Whether it is the Hindu, the Buddhist or Sikh or Jain or other religion, it does not look down on anybody. So long as we have belief in God and adhere to certain spiritual values, we will always be regarded as truly religious men. If we do not have it, however, much we may talk, however much we may read scriptures, we will not be considered truly religious men.

Our religion has moved from stage to stage—we had the *Vedas,* then we had the *Upaṇisads,* then we had the *Gitā;* then we had the *Ācharyās,* the *Bhaktas,* and today also we have people who belong to the real core of our religion. There are representatives of the true spirit of religion. We may not recognise them; but there are quite humble, unostentatious souls who are perpetually changing themselves, perpetually meditating, all the time trying to find out what is wrong with them and what they should do to make themselves worthy of the great traditions of our culture.

Every society has a soul as well as a body. These things help to make our bodies strong and at the same time we must do something to enrich our spirit if we are to sustain ourselves properly in this country or in the world. Both these aspects, the spiritual and the physical, constitute the nature of any society.

You find two sides in the Buddha's life, meditation, leading to the development of enlightenment, and service of humanity the rest of the time. These two, enlightenment and service, constitute the essentials of any religion. At the time of the Buddha, though there were teachers in our country who said that *atma jñana* or knowledge of the self is essential, more important than the mere performing of ceremony, etc., the most of humanity in this country were practising the rituals. Without the knowledge of the Reality which is enlightenment in our own nature, by doing outward rituals we do not understand the real significance of religion.

A man will have to think within himself, concentrate his attention and try to realise what is the Reality which is there, of which all these things are the expression. The Buddha was dissatisfied with the way in which religion was practised in those days and said, as another prophet says, 'We want mercy, not sacrifice'. We want real help, love of humanity. That is what we require and we do not require all other formulae and ritualistic ceremonies. He condemned rituals and made out that these rituals do not take us to the Ultimate Truth. If we want to attain the Truth, we will have to do exactly what the Buddha did.

He looked at the world, met the sights of a sick man, an old man, and a dead man. Death, old age, sickness, are the perils to which human flesh is exposed. Is there any way to get out of these things? He then met a *sādhu,* a monk, who was looking bright. He asked him, 'How is it, in this world so full of sorrow, that you are able to have an appearance of brightness?' The monk simply said: 'O, best of men, afraid of birth and death, I have become a monk, a wanderer, without any settled abode, to escape from the tyranny of Time.'

Time has for its symbol birth and death, and if you wish to overcome time, if you wish really to obtain *nirvāṇa*, that is merely escape from time; not escape from the time in the sense that we avoid temporal things but escape from subjection to time. *Nirvāṇa* is not only time-transcending, it is also time-transforming. After we attain enlightenment, we indulge in the affairs of the world by trying to transform, though we try to redeem time and make it eternity. It is not live in time with the proper perspective in our mind. That has been the gospel which the Buddha taught: escape from time and at the same time control over time. That is the way in which we have to live in this world and the rest of time we have to devote ourselves to the service of humanity.

His whole life is a succession of these two sides. Trying by every possible means to attain enlightenment; and once he became enlightened, he spent himself in the service of humanity. These two things, wisdom and love, they constitute the essence of every religion and the Buddha emphasised those two things in his life, gave us practical illustration that we have to live in this world to acquire wisdom and to spend our life in the service of humanity. That is what he attempted to do. So if you wish to know what constitutes the real essence of religion, it is illustrated by the life of the Buddha. His own career is there.

Unfortunately, so many other things have also come up and so many sects arose even in Buddhism. It became a scholastic, dogmatic and sectarian religion. We have to get back to the original purity, vigour and dynamism, all that the Buddha stood for. Each man must descend into the depth of his consciousness and discover there a permanent religion of which everything else is the expression; and once he has attained that kind of wisdom, he must be serving humanity.

Wisdom and love, these are the two things which should be regarded as constituting the essential aspects of the Buddha's religion. He said that life is suffering, and suffering has a cause, and we can escape from suffering and we can attain *nirvāṇa* or enlightenment. It is not something, which is beyond our scope. It is possible for us to attain *nirvāṇa* here and now. It is not essential for us to escape into another world. If we wish to become truly enlightened here and now by constant practice or deep meditation, it will be possibile for us to attain enlightenment.

When once we have that enlightenment, then we go out into the world; we do not withdraw from the world but we participate in it. We get involved in it; all the time we are working for the uplift of humanity. If this temple suggests to us, inspires us with these ideals of self-knowledge and love of humanity it will have done a useful service. It is for that that we go to a temple.

There is a verse which tells us that the right kind of religion is soaking yourself in the spirit of the Divine, in the spirit of the spiritual; the second way is by contemplation and meditation; if even that is not possible for you to do, you take to image worship; and if even that is not possible, you do *homa* and *yātrā:*

> *uttamā sahajā vasthā dvitīvyā dhyānadhāraṇā*
> *tritiyā pratimāpujā homayātrā caturthikā*
>
> The man who is possessed by God, who is a truly emancipated being, who is really divine, is one who lives constantly in the spirit of God, naturalises in the atmosphere of God; and not those who put on costumes and tell us they are the teachers.

A truly religious man has to perform things which cost him a lot, as the Buddha did; he gave up his palace, his kingdom, his wife, his child, because religious life is something that costs us enormously. It is not something which we can purchase from a grocery shop or a drug store. It is something which we can get by passing through stern discipline, by going through a travail of spirit. Most of us practise religion, go to temples, churches, etc., think that we are religious, but in our hearts all the time there are irreligious things. So, what is necessary is a process of establishing victory over the impediments to the insight into the Ultimate Reality. Achieve it by intellectual and spiritual struggle; you will be a different man and your works will have a greater value than what you are able to possess.

Man as a logical being is not a final end in human evolution; he is incomplete, imperfect, he has to grow into something higher.

CHAPTER 12

THE SPIRITUAL MIND

In my own lifetime, I have seen so many changes in the world of science—telephones, automobiles, radio, television, aeroplanes, etc. So much of scientific advance is taking place. In the three quarters of this century, work has been done which exceeds the volume of work done in the previous many centuries. It shows how our age is essentially an age of science and technology. In geology also many changes have taken place. Earthquakes, volcanoes, glaciers, wearing away of mountains, disappearance of rivers and change of direction, all of them are of great importance, though these events take long stretches of time to effect themselves. And it is also true that by the study of the rocks and fossils, what is called petrology and palaeontology, some speculation and theories have also, been advanced. We are saying that from the unicellular organism through the primate we have come to man. When life arrived, when consciousness comes into being in this world, these are questions which are directly related to investigations which scientists make.

We have a very early *Upanisad* which comes from the 8th century B.C. which talks about the cosmic evolution, and it puts down five steps in that cosmic ladder. First of all you have the inorganic, the physical so to say, then you have the biological, psychological, logical, then the mental, then the intellectual and then the spiritual. We have now reached the level of the logical mind, the conceptual mind, which dwells in abstractions, which builds cathedrals, temples, etc., but this is not the end of human evolution. This logical mind, has to grow into the spiritual. The intellectual concept give us ideas of race, of religion, of nation which makes us look upon people belonging to other religions and other nations as alien to ourselves.

There are these concepts which are developed by the logical mind of man, what is called *vijñana;* but it is said that this *vijñana* has to grow into *añanda* or the freedom of the human spirit when it rids itself of shibboleths, when it looks upon the whole world as kindred and makes for common fellowship. That is the idea to which we have to grow. It asserts that man as a logical being is not a final end in human evolution. He is incomplete, imperfect, he has to grow into something higher.

That is coming to us from the scientific side also. The minerals we get, the oils we get, the fuel which we use, these have been the lifeline of industrial development. Today we get the uranium also and this uranium is a means by which nuclear weapons can be made. How this nuclear energy is to be used, whether, it is for human betterment and progress or for the destruction of fellow human beings and the destruction of all the great arts and achievements which have been built by the hard work and toiling effort of human beings, how it is to happen depends on the spirit of man. This spirit of man has to grow. He has to evolve, he has to take a leap forward.

The human being as he is today, belonging to a particular group limited in its character, if he tries to develop chauvinistic nationalistic concepts, then this uranium which is dug out of the earth's crust may prove to be a disaster to humanity. But if it is to prove of benefit to humanity, it is essential for the human being to grow better. That is where the challenge thrown by the output of uranium on one side and the *Upanisadic* concept which tells us that man as an intellectual being is not enough, he is not the final product of evolution, both these things converge. If the challenge of our age is to be met, if this world is to grow into an earthly paradise where human beings can live in freedom, fellowship and friendship, if that is to happen, it is necessary for the human being himself to grow. So it is that we are called upon to use all the resources available to us for the purpose of perfecting ourselves.

This country, from the beginning of its history, has emphasised another direction of human development. If you look into the Indus Valley Civilisation you will find there the image of *mahayogi,* the great ascetic — a man wrapped in contemplation, trying to improve his own nature, trying to establish some kind of conquest over his own passions. You find again in the Buddha, who sits down under the Bodhi tree, trying to lacerate his body and torture his mind in quest of truth. He tells us, man has to suffer if he is to grow in his nature. Every kind of quest is related to a conquest; you must be heroic, you must be able to establish your own nature. When Jesus was by the side of the river Jordan, wrapped in prayer and meditation, he was again thinking of the improvement of human nature. So also Muhammad, when he climbed the mount at Mecca, trying to find out what the truth of things is. He is not outward bound, not looking at the earth, but he is trying to find out how human nature can be developed.

We have so many witnesses of this spirit, you may call it of spiritual discipline, the spirit of holiness. This is the spirit which was exalted by this country for the last fifty centuries, so far as our history goes.

Look at a man like Gandhi. He symbolizes the soul of India, the spirit of India. People came up to him and said, 'You are trying to win freedom for the country but look at history. History tells us no country has even own its freedom by the methods of truth and love as you suggest.' His answer was, 'Let us not follow the bad example of history. Let us set a good example by trying to achieve national freedom in this country by the methods of non-violence, non-hatred, friendship, *karuça, adroha, maitri'*. These are the ideas which he put before us.

So, from the time of the ancient Indus Valley Civilization down to Gandhi and Ramakrishna, you have one spirit, one kind of discipline which they exalted. To make our thoughts conform to spiritual wisdom, to make our will in accordance with the realisation of the universal purpose of fellowship, to mould our emotions into harmony with world unity, that is the great cosmic purpose, that is the will of the ages, it is the will of Providence, it is the meaning of history, that we should move forward to fellowship and friendship, to raise ourselves to higher spiritual status. That has been the lesson which this country has adopted and has given to the world also.

Even today we do not exalt military depots or industrial magnates. But a man in a loin-cloth, like Gandhi, or one like Vinoba walking barefoot from place to place, these are the people whom this country exalts. They are the examples to tell us that man in all his scientific glory is nothing comparable to a man who has established supremacy over his own nature. It is the Buddha who said, 'Victory breeds hatred, the conquered live in sorrow.' We should not aim at establishing any kind of material victory. Today, when the world is in a crisis, at a parting of the ways, when we are trying to find out how best we can harness these great nuclear powers, how we can use them for the development of human welfare and not for human destruction, it is the example which this country has put forward which we have to remember.

There are embodiments of holiness and sanctity in every part of the world. Therefore, it is nothing special, it is not the monopoly of this particular country. But we have now to come back to that. We have to realise that man is intended for self-fulfilment, he is not intended for self-destruction. So the great uranium deposits which we are able to get, from which we can make nuclear energy, these things will have to be utilised for the betterment of man, for making this world into a great whole which it is intended to be.

God meant us to love one another and to create. He did not mean us to hate one another and destroy ourselves. That is the parting of the ways. That is the crisis in which we are. And it is essential for the great international scientists to remember something of this spiritual dimension, which this country has exalted from the Indus Valley days down to Mahatma Gandhi. If you are able to do it, you will not only have enriched our material wealth and knowledge but you will have enriched the resources of humanity, the invisible forces of goodness which are there, latent in every human being, you will be able to bring them out, make them manifest.

It is said there is incarnation. That incarnation is not present in a few individuals. What a few individuals can do, the rest of humanity can also do. We must have the incarnation of the

Supreme in the whole human race. That is what we should attempt to do. Science has given us the facilities necessary. It has brought the world together, it has enabled us to understand the spiritual heritage of every nation, and if we can mobilise the spiritual resources of the whole world, if we are able to put them all into effect, it will be possible for us to make this world a better place than we have found it.

❑❑❑

Key for Diacritical Marks

Upaniṣada	a	=	अ	Pronounced as 'u' in cup.
Brāhman	ā	=	आ	Pronounced as 'a' in march.
Taittiriya	ai	=	ऐ	Pronounced as 'a' in cap.
Gauravāt	au	=	औ	Pronounced as 'ow' in brow.
Brahmā	b	=	ब	Pronounced as 'b' in bat.
Bhārat	bh	=	भ	Pronounced as 'bh' in Bhopal
Vācaspatī	c	=	च	Pronounced as 'ch' in church
Pucchḥai	chḥ	=	छ	Pronounced as 'chh' in Chhatisgarh.
Ātmavid	d	=	द्	Pronounced as 'th' in though.
Ādi	da	=	द	Pronounced as 'th' in the.
Ḍamru	ḍ	=	ड	Pronounced as 'd' in double.
Dharma	dh	=	ध	Pronounced as 'dh' in dhoti.
Veda	e	=	ए	Pronounced as 'e' in offend.
Granthān	g	=	ग	Pronounced as 'g' in grapes.
Ghanshyam	gh	=	घ	Pronounced as 'gh' in ghoul/ghost.
Mahāvira	h	=	ह	Pronounced as 'h' in hat.
Vidyā	i	=	इ	Pronounced as 'i' in inn.
Īśvara	ī	=	ई	Pronounced as 'ee' in creek.
Jina	j	=	ज	Pronounced as 'j' in jug.
Majjhima	jh	=	झ	Pronounced as 'jh' in Jhelum.
Jñāna	gya	=	ज्ञ	Pronounced as 'gya' in Borgia.
Akṛtaḥ	k	=	क	Pronounced as 'k' in kite.
Bhikhave	kh	=	ख	Pronounced as 'kh' in khan.
Cakṣuḥ	ḥ	=	अः	Pronounced as 'uhh' in uhh.
Lābhyo	l	=	ल	Pronounced as 'l' in lamp.

Grāhyam	m	=	म्	Pronounced as ‘m’ in camp.
Mantravid	ma	=	म	Pronounced as ‘m’ in madam.
Śaṁkara	ṁ	=	अं	Pronounced as ‘ung’ in clung.
Mantra	n	=	न्	Pronounced as ‘n’ in shrink.
Kṛtena	na	=	न	Pronounced as ‘n’ in nose.
Brāhmaṇa	ṇ	=	ण	Pronounced as ‘ṇ’ in varṇa.
Bodhi	o	=	ओ	Pronounced as ‘o’ in hoe.
Pratiloma	p	=	प	Pronounced as ‘p’ in pink.
Phalam	ph	=	फ	Pronounced as ‘f’ in full.
Shariq	q	=	क़	Pronounced as ‘que’ in oblique.
Sūtra	r	=	र्	Pronounced as ‘r’ in brown.
Guṇāśrayah	ra	=	र	Pronounced as ‘r’ in race.
Urhnā	rh	=	ड़	Pronounced as ‘rh’ in Rhodesia.
Muḍḥo	ḍḥ	=	ढ़	Pronounced as ‘rh’ in rhinoceros.
Ṛg	ṛ	=	ऋ	Pronounced as ‘ri’ in ring.
Yasya	s	=	स्	Pronounced as ‘s’ in swing.
Satya	sa	=	स	Pronounced as ‘s’ in subtle.
Śūdra	ś	=	श	Pronounced as ‘sh’ in shoe.
Viṣṇu	ṣ	=	ष	Pronounced as ‘sh’ in shingle.
Ātmā	t	=	त्	Pronounced as ‘t’ in mitre.
Sat	ta	=	त	Pronounced as ‘t’ in Dante.
Kuṭumbakam	ṭ	=	ट	Pronounced as ‘t’ in cricket.
Vṛthā	th	=	थ	Pronounced as ‘th’ in thought.
Kaṭḥa	ṭḥ	=	ठ	Pronounced as ‘ṭḥ’ in Thomas.
Anuloma	u	=	उ	Pronounced as ‘u’ in hue.
Svarūpa	ū	=	ऊ	Pronounced as ‘oo’ in scooter.
Mahāvīra	v	=	व्	Pronounced as ‘v’ in living.
Vacana	va	=	व	Pronounced as ‘v’ in live.
Aparoksha	ksh	=	क्ष	Pronounced as ‘ksh’ in kshatriya.
Cintaya	y	=	य	Pronounced as ‘y’ in yacht.
Phiroza	z	=	ज़	Pronounced as ‘z’ in Aurangzeb.